CORPORATE SOCIAL RESPONSIBILITY IN UK SUPERMARKET INDUSTRY

NAVEED QAZI

The author, having worldwide rights, ascertains the moral right to be associated with this work.

No part of this publication may be reproduced, distributed, or transmitted in any form, or by any means, including photocopying, recording, or other electronic or mechanical methods, without the prior written permission of the publisher, except in the case of brief quotations embodied in critical reviews, and certain other non-commercial uses, permitted by copyright law.

All rights reserved.

ISBN 13: 978-1985565487
ISBN-10: 198556548X

Formatting, proofreading and editing done by the author.
Typeset in Adobe Caslon Pro

www.naveedqazi.com

Cover design also by Naveed Qazi
Original photo by Clem Onojeghuo (Pexels.com)

Paperback and digital editions available from Kindle Direct Publishing, an Amazon unit.

UK | US | Australia | Italy | Spain | India | Netherlands
Japan | Brazil | Canada | Germany | Mexico | UAE
Singapore | Turkey | Poland | China | Saudi Arabia

kindle
direct
publishing

Copyright © 2018 Naveed Qazi

'It is not good enough to do what the law says. We need to be in the forefront of these (social responsibility) issues.'

Anders Dahlvig, CEO of IKEA, quoted in Financial Times.

Contents

Executive Summary
Introduction
Objectives of Research
Review of CSR Literature
CSR as a strategic activity
Stakeholder Theory
Caroll's Pyramid of Social Responsibilities
Triple P Bottom line (People, Profit, Planet)
Competitive Advantage: Porter's Theory of CSR
Theory of Corporate Constitutionalism
Integrative Social Contract Theory
Adversarial view of CSR
Virtue Ethics
Deontological Ethics
Consequentialist Ethics
Environmental Ethics
Corporate Philanthropy
Corporate Citizenship
Research Methodology
Research Findings
Research Case I
Ascertaining the performance of environmental reporting by researching into carbon emission reduction, improving energy efficiency, packaging, and waste management initiatives in the last five years
Asda Ltd.
Tesco Ltd.
Waitrose Ltd.
Sainsbury's Ltd.
A Comparative Analysis
Research Case II
Determining how the supermarket industry applies sustainable policies of corporate philanthropy through local community development

Asda Ltd.
Tesco Ltd.
Waitrose Ltd.
Sainsbury's Ltd.
A Comparative Analysis
Research Case III
Enquiring responsible sourcing of food products in UK CSR industry through ethical trading standards
Asda Ltd.
Tesco Ltd.
Waitrose Ltd.
Sainsbury's Ltd.
A Comparative Analysis
Conclusion
Personal Reflections
References

Acknowledgements

I want to thank my supervisor, Mary Deuchar, who guided me, throughout the dissertation process. Without her important suggestions, and guidelines, this research work would not have been possible.

She always followed a progressive guiding approach as supervision.

I also want to thank my parents and friends, for their appreciation.

Executive Summary

This book was basically a dissertation, written for MSc International Business course, at the University of Hertfordshire, about Corporate Social Responsibility, in the hyper-supermarket sector, of the United Kingdom.

The research found out that leading supermarkets, in the UK, have taken corporate social responsibility seriously.

The research objectives were made through a project-based research approach, on four companies, namely *Asda, Tesco, Waitrose, and Sainsbury's*.

The research contains significant comparative analysis, for each research objective.

The comparative analysis had been qualitative, and devoid of any comparative numerical analysis, due to insignificant data available, at that moment in time.

The research methodology had been based, on secondary research, due to time considerations, and the nature of the research.

Company specific CSR reports were mainly used for the research methodology.

The reason given for that is that it made full use of the already published research, through CSR reports, found in archives, through official websites of retail companies.

Google search, by finding relevant articles, was done, and it proved significant for the research, and provided the basis, for research objectives.

The research findings have set the basis for technological improvements, as a pivotal initiative to enhance environmental sustainability, to reduce carbon emissions, on roads, as well as inside the refrigeration facilities, of the supermarkets.

The research has also suggested innovative ways in developing newer designs, of the supermarket buildings, so that more eco-friendly stores pave the way for the future.

It has also been concluded that there is a creative management necessary, for waste management initiatives. All these factors have likely resulted as new ventures, for retail supermarkets, for CSR, in United Kingdom.

The dissertation also talks about the important aspects of corporate philanthropy, and the need for local community development, through business establishments, in United Kingdom.

The book argues that CSR and philanthropy go hand in hand, and form important considerations, for the reputational, and moral value, of the businesses.

The research also shows the patterns of investments, of the supermarkets, in the local community matters. The research has found out that philanthropy, for health causes, has been the most important pattern of investment, in recent years.

This talks volumes about the way businesses are changing their perceptions, by implementing philanthropy, and showing a relationship between business, and the society.

The final objective is research about ethical sourcing of

food. The findings suggest that sourcing with integrity, through a code of conduct, has been the main aspect of ethical sourcing, in United Kingdom supermarket retail industry.

Getting accreditations from top bodies associated with farming has been another way of enhancing better consumer response on food related products.

This initiative has been taken as a top CSR priority, by four researched supermarket companies, alongside soil research for quality harvesting.

Introduction

According to Iles (2004), UK retailers are developing broad based accountability systems, so that there can be some kind of sustainability, in their operations. UK retailers, are increasing quantifying their environmental footprints, and producing more corporate reports.

British retailers have been suggesting a dialogue process, as listening to civil society actors, as well as workers, suppliers, and producers.

They are also including discussions with farmers, participation in benchmarking, partnerships, with environmental organisations, and projects, in communities, such as Tesco and Sainsbury's.

UK retailers are also reviewing the trends, in politics, to critique the markets that are trying to implement CSR.

The retailers are improving resource use, reducing energy, and putting higher transparency within the UK market.

Some British retailers have started on long-term affiliations, such as unfinished future projects, ranging from fair trade, biodiversity, pesticides, and environmental developments, in United Kingdom.

According to Mintel (2001), Tesco dominates the sector with the market share, but *Asda* is gaining shoppers, in terms of weekly shoppers.

Sainsbury's on the other hand, has responded to recession well, and had led its emphasis, on value end of its offer, but with compromising brand strengths.
As per Jones et al. (2005), there has been an increasing

pressure within the past decade, which include a variety of factors, such as, increasing consumer awareness, pressure from government, trade unions, and investors, new legislation, developments, in information, and communication technologies, and media attention that has forced a number of CSR retailers, in UK, to impact their activities.

British Retail Consortium (BRC) has suggested that it marks an important milestone for the retail industry, and has stressed its members, for many national sustainability initiatives. There was also a government's approach to introduce CSR, in UK, so that 'everyone should have a higher quality of life'.

DEFRA (Department for Environment, Food and Rural Affairs) made a review of progress, across three pillars of sustainable development, and focused on issues, such as waste management, and reduction of road traffic.

UK grocery market has grown from 93.3 billion in 1998, to 146.3 billion, in 2008. *Tesco* has around (28%) of the market share, followed by *Asda* (15.2%), *Sainsbury's* (14.3%), and finally, followed by *Waitrose*, which has a market share of around (3.5%) It is also claimed that UK grocery market is one of the most sophisticated, in terms of private labels (Li, 2008).

UK retail is said to harbour the greatest concentration of retail power, anywhere in the world (Morgan & Monley, 2002).

Michael (2004) even concedes to the point that UK has transformed, from a nation of shopkeepers, to innumerable markets, to a supermarket culture, dominated by a handful of large supermarket retailers.

This also led in opening of the office of fair-trading, where retailers, such as *Tesco, Asda, and Sainsbury's,* have built up a dominance, in the food retailing, over the past sixty years (BBC, 2006).

In 2006 alone, the top three retailers namely *Tesco, Asda, Sainsbury's* held around seventy-two per cent, of the market share, alone.

Tesco argues that CSR is an important part of the entire approach to business, from Board level to checkout. *Sainsbury's* on the other hand, charges six board level directors, with responsibility for individual CSR issues.

Also, all the large food retailers are committed in attracting and retaining a culturally, and socially diverse workforce, with emphasis on meeting the best people, and meeting the needs of the communities, in which they trade.

Jones et al. (2006) states that retailers, particularly supermarkets in UK are much more active, in using CSR themes, on promotional television screens, leaflets and posters.

Objectives of Research

The main objectives are to assess CSR policies in the supermarket sector of United Kingdom.

They are classified as:

- Ascertaining the performance of environmental reporting by researching into carbon emission reduction, improving energy use, packaging, and waste management initiatives in the last five years.

- Determining how the supermarket industry in the UK applies sustainable policies through local community development.

- Inquiring into responsible sourcing of food products which are traded through ethical farming standards.

Research would be done, regarding the targets of carbon emission, of the top four retail companies, namely *Asda, Sainsbury's, Waitrose,* and *Tesco*.

Data collection would also be done, regarding how the said companies are improving upon energy efficiency, in terms of refrigeration leaks, and the strategy for waste management initiatives. Environmental impacts will be identified.

Another objective is to determine the community involvement, of the four mentioned retail companies, so that patterns of investment, for local community, will be identified, for suitable conclusions.

Review of CSR Literature

CSR as a Strategic Activity

According to Louche et al. (2010), CSR has a potential to become a strategic activity, provided if it adds value, to various dimensions of business, including society and eco-systems.

The first condition is that CSR needs to become integrated, with the strategy of the firm.
The second condition is that strategic CSR should have the means to measure and monitor new or additional values created.

As per Galbreath (2009), CSR should be strategised, on what company is trying to achieve, which takes several expectations, into consideration, such as industry and competence.

Hence, there exists a likely link between CSR and strategy, through integration, of the mentioned core elements, such as resources, and market needs, with CSR, that operate, in the business environment.

It can also be said that the level of CSR should also be compatible with the firm's mission.

Source: Galbreath (2009)

According to Louche et al. (2010), CSR is closely related to transparency, accountability, and legitimacy, that act according to public interests. Strategic CSR integrates stakeholders concerns into firm's strategy.

It relies on the concept of mutual dependence, of firms, and society. It implies that any business decision, as well as the policy decision, influences society, its stakeholders as well as the businesses.

As a result, firms no longer strive for financial benefits

in isolation, but adopt a broader view including environmental and social benefits.

In strategic CSR, the voice of the stakeholder is inserted through continual interaction. It can be said that CSR creates relations between society and business, and it is harder for businesses to sustain, if they do not recognise the benefits of CSR. It may also enhance the business performance of the business through CSR motives.

According to Baron (2001), CSR influences 'integrated market and non – market strategy' that in turn influences firm's competitive position. It is a tool that helps to control activism of stakeholders through positive action.
As per Louche et al. (2010), strategic CSR comprising of stages including market crystallisation, market expansion, competitive turbulence, and absorption.

Market crystallisation is introduced through focused efforts of CSR, by few companies, to develop the market, which pave the way for market expansion.

It leads towards greater stakeholder awareness, leading to a stage of competitive turbulence, which raises the bar of increasing stakeholder expectations, leading towards the absorption phase, where only competitive companies get rewarded.

Primary CSR occurs when a firm does not seek a payback, and secondary CSR occurs as a part of firm's normal commercial routine. Sometimes, firms may engage in both types of behaviour simultaneously.

Hence, it can be ascertained that it becomes necessary to distinguish between primary and secondary CSR behaviour when considering strategic activities, and a higher performance is needed, to satisfy stakeholders.

It can also be said that CSR revolves around stakeholder awareness, and expectations, based on a life cycle of repetitive phases.

According to Burke & Logsdon (1996), there is a need to create social strategies. With the result environment scanning and monitoring have become importance by the advent of strategic CSR strategies.

Centrality of firm's closeness to strategic fit, specificity by manufacturing scope for decision making, visibility of stakeholders for the firm, through capturing benefits, proactivity in overseeing social trends, voluntarism by manufacturing scope for decision making, ultimately result in the creation of value driven activities for the firm.

As per Louche et al. (2010), strategic CSR aims to promote a long-term vision of business accountability, to a wide range of stakeholders. The objective of strategic CSR is to generate brand loyalty and improving societal demands.

In this process, 'strategic fit' also plays a role in the implementation of a successful CSR programme because there needs to be an alignment, between values of the company, and values of the CSR programme.

While strategic CSR aims to develop a competitive advantage, it is ascertained that the role of regulation carries importance. Regulation both has positive as well as negative impacts, for business. Strict environmental regulation has a negative impact on economic wealth, but a positive effect on consumer welfare.

However, sustained innovation through regulatory measures may have a positive impact in the longer term.

Therefore, it can be said that regulation paves the way for the evolution of CSR in the business operations. It can also be ascertained that the impact of CSR on business is directly proportional to the type of regulation.

Another point, which can be discussed, is that the strategic CSR can prove beneficial, as it likely promotes the long-term vision of business accountability to a wide range of shareholders. Recent literature has linked CSR with strategy of the firm.

In keeping the dissertation objectives in mind, the role of regulation in strategic CSR context will carry importance in terms of carbon emission reduction, and the need to create competitive advantages in keeping societal needs in consideration, through ethical farming, philanthropy, and educative strategies.

Strategic CSR has implications on many stakeholders and it can likely create positive long-term implications for the society

Stakeholder Theory

According to Keinert (2008), stakeholder theory is the first economic theory, advocating a departure, from the classical, hitherto, largely undisputed primate of shareholder rights in the 1970's.

It demanded a relationship between society, business, firms, and their dependency on the society surrounding it. The pioneer of stakeholder theory, Freeman (1984), states the needs of shareholders, but also of the other groups concerned by corporate activity, known as stakeholders, which are to be met, or at least considered by the corporation.

The groups concerned can be both external and internal, thereby including employees, executives, suppliers, consumers, but also environment and society, at large. Therefore, it can be said that stakeholder theory considers corporate vision, strategy and tactics to people, or groups other than shareholders of the firm, for value maximisation.

This notion likely fits with the dissertation objectives, in the sense that UK retail companies looking for philanthropy, and environmental concerns, may please stakeholders, such as local community councils, consumers, and environmental activists.

According to Fontaine et al. (2006), stakeholder theory is giving business broader responsibilities. The decision taken by firms should also ensure its survival, while considering stakeholders. It is also ascertained that managers are responsible for stakeholder management, and by engaging stakeholders, managers want to increase shareholder value.

As per Keinert (2008), stakeholders are defined as social groups that affect or are affected by firm's actions, or have an interest, right, claim or ownership in an organisation. Management, according to stakeholder theory, carries fiduciary duties, towards the various constituencies and its task therefore is the reconciliation of competing stakeholder demands.

Therefore, it can be ascertained that by engaging stakeholders, managers of the firm can create new opportunities and strategic directions. It can also be said that contribution of literature regarding stakeholder participation has given rise to CSR strategies.

According to Cooper (2004), stakeholder theory can be justified on three aspects namely the 'descriptive accuracy', 'instrumental power', and 'normative validity'.

Descriptive accuracy suggests that when considering stakeholder theory from a managerial perspective, and when attempting to develop an accurate stakeholder theory, stakeholder identification becomes important. Instrumental power of stakeholder theory suggests that stakeholder management can be used to achieve shareholder value, and the balance between the different shareholder groups interest is essential in ensuring that the organisation continues to be viable and achieves other performance goals.

Normative validity raises a critical issue regarding what is ethical and what is moral behaviour. The actual moral and ethical models used in conjunction with stakeholder theory include Kantian ethics, social contract, the common good and Aristotelian ethics.

As per Donaldson and Preston (1995), stakeholder theory has also represented a controversial approach among market capitalist economies.

Therefore, it can be ascertained that a competitive advantage will follow if there is a trust and co-operation between the organisations and stakeholders. It is also observed that the three aspects of stakeholder theory are mutually supportive of each other, while creating an argument for long implications for business decisions through obliging towards stakeholder demands of moral and ethical value.

Hence, it can be said that transparency, moral enhancement, and sustainability should likely arise while applying stakeholder considerations through its theoretical aspects. The whole debate regarding stakeholder management presents foundations, for CSR in business.

According to Keinert (2008), stakeholder relations can sometimes be compatible, while sometimes, it can oppose each other. It is ascertained that the overall goal through stakeholder management should be maximum co-operation between stakeholder groups and the objectives of the co-operation. Stakeholder theory suggests that corporations cause tremendous social effects, on the society, through markets. Therefore, the firm should decide on the stakeholder management according to priorities as different corporations will respond to different stakeholders differently.

Hence, identified primary and secondary shareholders will be responsible in creating good or bad relationships between stakeholders and the corporates. These steps will likely create a corporate as a dominant social institution.

These positives are related to my dissertation because modern theorists have maintained some sort of relationship with stakeholders, which can help in rigorous analysis in achieving the objectives, pertaining to CSR.

Caroll's Pyramid of Social Responsibilities

Pyramid of Social Responsibility by Caroll (1991) is the most valuable theory, concerning the actual content of a firm's social responsibility. It states that the firm's responsibility of economic nature is a primary obligation.

However, it also ascertains that the corporations should

legitimately pursue growth, and provide society with goods and services at 'fair prices.' Moving up the pyramid, Caroll identifies legal, ethical and philanthropic responsibilities that a company should face next to its economic responsibilities.

Legal responsibilities are regarded as *codified ethics*, coexisting with economic responsibilities.

Ethical responsibilities are offshoots of business ethics movement, that are raising the bar for legal responsibilities, and placing higher expectations, on business leaders.

Philanthropic responsibilities, on the other hand, are those corporate actions that make businesses act like good corporate citizens.

Therefore, it can be ascertained that the pyramid consists of certain levels that distinguishes between mandatory, and voluntary responsibilities.

Figure two shows the levels of Pyramid of Social Responsibilities

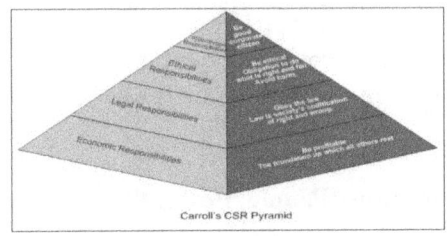

Source: Fontaine et al. (2006)

According to Griseri & Seppala (2010), the responsibilities presented in the pyramid are in not any way cumulative, or consecutive, but are mutually exclusive.

Therefore, it may be possible that the company fulfils the ethical expectations, but fails to meet the legal responsibilities. This model of CSR helps to distinguish and clarify the 'motives' and 'contradictions' behind corporate behaviour.

However, the pyramid does not 'predict' the corporate behaviour, or indicate priorities for decision-making. The four-part model has, therefore, likely been successful, in encompassing a range of concerns, and definitions, of social responsibility. Therefore, it can be said that the economic responsibilities are the broadest, and the most encompassing, in scope.

It can also be suggested that the tip of the pyramid, namely the discretionary and philanthropic responsibilities are the narrowest in scope, and are thus voluntary in responsibilities.

However, it can further be ascertained that Caroll's major theoretical achievement is to show that social responsibilities are to be considered by corporations, independent of what is legally required.

Therefore, ethics and a sense of moral responsibility is the stimulus required by companies to remove problems from the society.

The Triple P Bottom Line (People, Profit, Planet)

According to Norman & Macdonald (2004), the notion of The Triple P Bottom line (People, Profit, Planet) suggests that corporation's ultimate success can not only be measured by financial bottom line, but also by ethical, societal, and environmental performance. It is also put forward that key stakeholders should be valued in business decision-making. The notion also maintains that overall fulfilment of responsibilities to stakeholders should be measured, calculated audited or recorded.

As per Keinert (2008), the 'Triple P Bottom line', affirms the pursuit of profits that form an important component of business, but in the meantime, the care for environment and social concerns constitute underestimated, but equally important dimensions.

In other words, the firm is a value creating entity. The firm should not only be dedicated to generating economic value, but it should also strive for value creation, concerning human beings, in or outside the corporation, as well as caring for the natural environment.

It also states that to prosper over the long term, a corporation must continuously meet society's needs, for goods and services, without destroying natural or social capital.

Therefore, it can be said that pursuit of profit should not be the sole purpose of any business, not at least, at the cost of environment or communities, because business decisions can have many bad implications at times.

Competitive Advantage: Porter's Theory of CSR

According to Porter & Kramer (2002), CSR is of outmost strategic importance, as corporate philanthropy, can often be the most cost-effective way, to improve the competitive context, if used wisely.

It is also suggested that a positive relationship between CSR and business opportunities in terms of market opportunities, productivity, and human competence, can be detected, and if exploited, can improve the quality of the business environment, both, in the home market, and abroad, where the multinationals operate.

It is further ascertained that for drawing competitive advantage out of CSR engagement is to avoid ad-hoc piecemeal, or dispersed, or unfocussed donating.

The mistake, which business leaders make is to 'do good', without taking the core considerations of business, competencies, and strategies.

Therefore, it can be suggested that well-elaborated and meaningful CSR programs, help to serve strategic goal, future needs, and exercise positive influence, and goodwill for the corporation. The social issues should be supported, in line, with the main business philosophy of the corporate. According to Porter & Kramer (2006), another source of major competitive advantage possibly achievable through CSR is the lowering of operational costs.

Apart from that, investments in environment friendly, or otherwise socially beneficial business processes, or products can incur incredible cost advantages, in case, when they later become either regulated, or an industry standard.

Therefore, CSR can also give competitive advantages to the firm, through positive publicity, and enhanced reputation. Hence, this notion, when compared to dissertation objectives will help to understand whether the mission of firms, in UK retail sector, lies in conjunction with CSR, concentrated on focused, and strategic donating, to reap benefits of competitive advantages, in the UK retail market.

Theory of Corporate Constitutionalism

According to Garriga & Mele (2004), the theory of corporate constitutionalism, put forward by Davis (1960), explores the role of power, in business, and the impact it has, on society.

The theory regards that business is a social institution, and it must use its power responsibly.

According to Crane et al. (2008), the causes that generate social power, of the firm, are not solely internal, but are also external. Their locus is shifting from the economic, the social forum, and the political forum, and vice versa.

Davis (1960) has also attacked the assumption of the classical economic theory, of perfect competition, that precludes the involvement of the firm, in society, besides creation of wealth. He formed the 'iron law of responsibility', and believed that companies, who do not use social power responsibly, will lose it, because other groups will eventually take that responsibility.

Personally, I believe that if the firms do not use social power responsibly, they will tend to lose it, because society demands certain responsibilities from businesses. Hence, the organisations, and business managers, have the discretion to define conditions, for power, for its responsible use.

It can also be said that power should be channelled, in a constructive way that paves the way for productive business, rather than acting an advocate for unreasonable power.

When related to dissertation objectives, the role of power, in devising CSR strategies, in UK retail market, will carry importance, as it will also depict the market position, of the companies, to pursue societal responsibilities.

Integrative Social Contract Theory

This theory is put forward by Donaldson & Dunfee (1994), and it considers business and society relationship, from the social contract tradition, mainly from the philosophical thought of Locke. He assumed that a sort of implicit social contract, between business and society, truly exists. This social contract implies some indirect obligation of business towards the society.

According to Crane et al. (2008), this theory considers the social, cultural, empirical, and normative aspects of management. Social responsibility comes from this consent. Firstly, there is a theoretical macro social contract appealing to all rational contractors. Secondly, there is a real micro social contract by members of numerous localised communities.

This theory offers a process, in which contracts, among industries and economic departments, can be legitimate. The macro social contract provides rules, for any social contracting. These rules are called 'hyper norms,' which are fundamental, and observable, in convergence with political, religious, and philosophical thought, in business.

Therefore, it can be said that a contract between business and society seems to exist. The management of the business ought to build societal considerations, for business.

For dissertation objectives, it can help to justify the societal implications, regarding what the UK retail sector is doing, for the communities.

Adversarial View of CSR

Many academics have presented arguments against CSR. Milton Friedman advanced the idea of shareholder value, being in conflict, with the notion of Corporate Social Responsibility.

According to him, companies are misusing their resources whenever they engage in CSR driven activities. He believes that social involvement is costly and may dilute the companies (Griseri & Seppala 2010).

As per Crane et al. (2010), CSR has been disdained as a giant public relation campaign, that is 'full of rhetoric', and not associated with any 'action'. Noam Chomsky, on the other hand, argues that corporations use CSR, as advertising, to mold consumer's desires, and act in a socially responsible way, only for their own benefit (Corporate Watch, 2012).

According to Griseri & Seppala (2010), the other idea given against CSR engagement is while companies may possess significant competences, they lack specific knowledge, skills and experience needed to deal with societal problems.

'A lack of accountability' viewpoint is also put forward by anti-CSR theorists, who state that public cannot hold company's accountable, same way, as the governments should be.

Therefore, it can be said that anti-CSR theorists argue that companies concentrate on economic activities, rather than performing other roles, in the society.
The proponents of this view might undermine democracy, by arguing that it is the responsibility of governments, to

mend laws, that allow companies to behave responsibly, at the first place.

Hence, it can be further ascertained that governments should control markets but only for the benefit of the society, and not only just for corporations.

With respect to dissertation objectives, it will be necessary to evaluate how corporate philanthropy, carbon emission reduction, and ethical farming standards, run in accordance with the government laws, that would result in socially responsible investments, and environmental performance.

Virtue Ethics

According to Griseri & Seppala (2010), virtue ethics are often traced in the writings of Aristotle and Confucius.

Managerial integrity showing appropriate behavioural traits, like honesty, kindness, fairness, and prudence, are traditionally associated with virtue ethics, in business.

A virtue does not compel a businessperson, to act in a certain way. It rather recommends them to do so. There also needs to be a strict distinction, between a manager being virtuous, or displaying certain specific virtues.

If character is what is important in business, then the development of professionals, and managers, in terms of kinds of judgments, they make, the kinds of attitudes they hold, becomes an important organisational goal. Equally, organisational cultures that reflect a virtue-ethical orientation are likely to focus less, on blame for actions, and focus more on self-evaluation for character.

There also needs to be coherence, in the values of

organisations, and the values inherent, in the goods and services. Therefore, it can be said that virtue ethics aims not to explain what our ethical attitudes are, but to change these in a certain direction.

Hence, there are many advantages to consider someone's character in business when thinking of ethics in business. It can also be suggested that there is a potential linkage between CSR and virtue ethics because moral traits form the basis of CSR functions.

It can help in understanding the foundations of the organisational culture, and managerial perspectives, regarding virtues in UK retail business, that is, to what extend is the retail sector honest, in showing records, of CO emission reduction, philanthropy, and community development.

Deontological Ethics

Deontology is derived from a Greek term for 'duty', and 'explanation.' The best-known example of deontological theory of ethics is that of the 18th century philosopher, Immanuel Kant.

His focus of ethics is to what humans can be fully responsible for, which is quite essential for our motives and actions.

This theory, when related to business, contains a straightforward test, for any business individual, that is, whether to act in the personal interests, or whether to act, for the principles of business. It requires managers and professionals to care about what their duty is.

Much business decision-making is founded on uncritical

acceptance of organisational goals, and on aims defined by classical microeconomics, which rely on universal pursuit of self-interest (Griseri & Seppala, 2010).

Therefore, this theory states that if managers really want to be effective, they should have a keen sense of rightness and wrongness.

In my opinion, the theory will help to explain what is it to be ethically right, and this test would become a tool for decision makers. The morality of the retail companies in the UK pursuing CSR initiatives would ultimately depend upon their actions.

CSR strategy, the main objectives, and organisation culture of retail companies, would provide the basis for deontological ethics.

Consequentialist Ethics

This theory suggests that the ethics of an action is to be evaluated, in terms of the consequences, it carries. It relies on an assumption that there is a solution to every ethical problem, and the individual can always find a choice, that is best available, in the circumstances. The theory further suggests that an action is considered good, if it does good, for greatest number of people (Griseri & Seppala, 2010).

Hence, in terms of business, managers need to use a wide range of decision strategies, each of which is suit the circumstances, to have positive implications, for their business decisions, on the stakeholders. Therefore, if retail companies are pursuing handful of CSR activities, the common good will be recognised, only if they pursue concerns, of the community, and society. Only then the principle of consequentialist ethics would apply.

Environmental Ethics

Environmental ethics has a significant influence, on the corporate behaviour, and has thought to be of moral consideration. The underlying theories of environmental ethics can still be classified, as a part of consequentialist, or other ethical traditions. These kinds of ethics have also allowed sustainability, to be seen, as an ethical issue, something that demands that we extend ideas of moral consideration, in terms of space and time (Murray & Blowfield, 2008).

There is a need to integrate a sound business strategy, with environmental philosophy. Corporations must consider the integrity of natural environment, and to incorporate environmental ethics, in the workings, of the profitable firm.

The companies need to understand sensitive co-operation with environment, to enhance productivity of the firm, to take advantage of the opportunities, to be environmentally ethical (Griseri & Seppala, 2010).

One environmental approach is the 'bright green' approach that states the drivers, for the necessary social change, to achieve sustainability, are technological in nature. This approach believes that new technologies, better design, and alternative forms of social organisation, can resolve the current environmental problems.

Therefore, I believe that CSR focus should be vital for environmental improvements. Arguments that have developed on environmental sustainability, are likely imperative for nations, to develop economically.

When keeping the dissertation objectives, into

consideration, it would be necessary to evaluate the extend of environmental performance, in terms of carbon emission reduction, the strategy of waste management, and energy efficiency, which can contribute towards environment friendliness, in the United Kingdom, through corporate functions.

Corporate Philanthropy

According to Keinert (2008), corporate social responsibility in terms of corporate philanthropy, is aimed to design value, for the firms.

Through cause related strategies, corporate philanthropy helps to create a corporate image, and identity, for the enterprise. It also helps to create goodwill, and a competitive advantage, for the enterprise, through regular donations, and cause related sponsorships.

It is an idea of giving something back to the society. Some companies also give their pretax incomes to arts, community investment, and educational causes. Companies even take a strategic view of philanthropy, by seeking out for causes, that are aligned to their business goals (Murray & Blowfield, 2008).

According to Crane et al. (2008), Porter's and Kramer's model of competitive advantage states that the philanthropic investments, by members of cluster can have a significant effect, on firm's competitiveness, and the performance, of all constituent companies.

It is ascertained that corporate philanthropy is sometimes the only way to improve competitive contexts.

It helps the companies to not only leverage their resources, but also existing efforts, and infrastructure of non-profits, and other institutions. Either individually or collectively, it can have a powerful effect, on the cluster's competitiveness, and the performance of all its constituent companies.

However, when corporate philanthropy does not create strategic philanthropic engagements, it generates bad media publicity, activist protests, and boycott.

Therefore, I believe that corporate philanthropy, through strategic ventures, should aim at giving a social impact, rather than mere publicity. True strategic charitable ventures can address important social and economic goals, simultaneously, targeting areas, where the company and society, are both, at a benefit.

In context of my dissertation objectives, companies should address corporate philanthropy, by merging the economic gains, of corporate philanthropy, through a right strategy, aiming at social investments, and shareholder's interest.

Retail companies, in the UK, should identify the sectors, for local community development, that would prove beneficial, for societal development, rather than mere publicity.

It would be also important to note that CSR ventures are not taken as a marketing tool, under the guise of corporate philanthropy.

Corporate Citizenship

Due to deregulation, and decreasing costs of technological improvements, some large multinational companies have greater economic, and social power than some governments. The concept of corporate citizenship is related to the sense of belongingness, within the community.

Crane et al. (2008) states that this concept overlaps with corporate philanthropy, social investments, and other responsibilities in business. It is ascertained that corporations enter the arena of corporate citizenship, at the point of government failure, in protection of citizenship. This view also acknowledges that some corporations have gradually come, to replace the most powerful institution, in the traditional concept of citizenship, namely the government.

The term 'Good Corporate Citizenship' is deemed to be defined, as an active community involvement. Corporations voluntarily assume responsibilities, as a major actor, within the society, by contributing to the enhancement, of the community life, through participative, and organised involvement.

However, corporations are also free in determining whether they want to proactively engage in these activities. If they do, they may experience substantial positive effects in financial performance, provided the engagement is in convergence with their strategic goals (Keinert, 2008).

Macintosh et al. (1998) states that business is regarded, as the engine of the society, where shareholders are the primary claimants, and stakeholders are the secondary claimants. It is an idea that has ethical dimensions such as risk avoidance, reinforcing relationships between individuals and communities, and setting standards for products and suppliers for better business competence.

In relation to dissertation objectives, I think that the concept of corporate citizenship, in relation to UK retail companies, should assume the role of engaging in profitable economic activities.

UK supermarket business should have a moral and responsible activity, which directly has an obligation towards social betterment. The board of directors, of these retail companies, should put themselves, on a mission, in serving social interests.

This evaluation, from literature, would prove beneficial, towards the development of research objectives.

Research Methodology

I will be mainly using:

- CSR reports of companies in the UK supermarket industry.
-Relevant press articles which give information of the emergence of CSR   strategy in UK supermarket.

CSR reports of the four retail companies, namely *Asda, Tesco, Waitrose, and Sainsbury* will be used. Internet will be used as an information gateway to collect data. All the necessary data, whether in raw or summarised form, would be extracted qualitatively, to develop the research findings.

Press coverage of the mentioned retail companies will also be used for data collection, to answer the research objectives. An Internet search using key search words 'Corporate Social Responsibility' plus the name of the 'retailer' will be used.

CSR reports are mostly of internal nature, which are then published externally, for the public for research, and marketing use. There are archives of CSR reports, stored on the official websites, of large UK retail companies.

I will be using the most recent CSR data, so that the data collected, would be up to date, for analysis, of large UK supermarket. They run into 20-30 pages, and contain much key information, about the financial, social, and marketing performance, of the companies.

In that sense, I will be collecting the relevant consolidated data, from these retail companies.

An inductive approach will be used, so that I understand the meaning of the data collected, and will summarise it, using comparative analysis. As the data is already available, on the Internet, it can likely help, in the analysis, of unseen situations, or unexpected new discoveries, through analysing the market situation, in UK retail.

Therefore, the whole research process should have an acceptable research design, so that it has a definite relevance, for the dissertation project.

The reason I will not be using deductive approach, is mainly because there is a need to create samples of sufficient size, through primary data, that would mainly involve collection of quantitative data.

That process would be time consuming and the nature of the research will be against following a deductive approach.

Also, the quality of my primary data analysis depends upon the knowledge of the managers or the staff. Therefore, already collected data through CSR reports, would likely prove beneficial, in answering of the research questions.

CSR reports are divided into different chapters and

relevant information would be extracted. It will be important, in the sense, that the data collected is properly categorized, for drawing suitable conclusions.

The press coverage will also be taken from official *Tesco, Waitrose, Sainsbury's,* and *Asda* websites.

The reason I will not be giving first preference, to the news media websites, is because the official websites, of these retail companies, have already collected the data, through outside press. Therefore, data collection becomes easier.

For example, when doing a search on their official websites namely *'Greener Tesco', 'Waitrose Press Centre', 'Sainsbury's PLC'*, several number of articles, and postings come up. Relevant amount of data, extracted from there, provides a base for developing dissertation objectives.

I will also ensure that unwanted data, such as case studies, which are irrelevant, in answering research questions, are excluded so that efficient data, in the remains for the analysis, to answer my research questions.

Hence, it will help me to interpret the credibility of the data collected. As there will be a heavy reliance, on company websites and CSR reports, it will also be important to analyse, whether any bias is emerging from the collection of data. Bias can be kept to a minimum through cross checking, of the collected data, through Google search.

My research methodology will be using external sources, such as press coverage of news websites. 'Google Scholar' yielded 31,300 results on a search regarding 'Corporate Social Responsibility and Supermarkets'. Therefore, relevant amount of information would be extracted from journal articles in writing a suitable introduction.

As my dissertation objectives are comparative in nature, multiple external sources like grocery and philanthropic websites for data analysis will be used.
I will be doing a cross-sectional analysis, so that I compare findings, and identify the points of differences, and similarities, in the trends, that are occurring, in large UK retail market. Hence, the whole process in developing the research context will be important.

My dissertation objectives are purely based on secondary data research, due to time and access constraints, when keeping the nature of research objectives into consideration.

There are various problems that could occur while collecting primary data such as:

- Authorisation to data collection from retail companies

- Office load

- Management laws

- Corporate bureaucracy

The above factors make secondary data collection likely a reliable process.
Hence questionnaires and interviews would likely prove insignificant, in compiling information necessary, to fulfil the objectives, considering the nature of the research, and problems associated, in compiling the primary data.

Therefore, secondary data analysis will be used, to collect the data, in a convenient format, for further processing, due to availability of information electronically. There are considerable advantages of cost, human and capital savings, when secondary data is used.

The large quantity of secondary data available online, regarding CSR in UK retail market, would help, in developing new insights, about the data collected.

Hence, right amount of judgment will be necessary, when using secondary data, because my choice of research question suit with secondary data analysis.

It is because there is a right amount of the breadth of data available, for CSR, in large super markets, in UK.

This gives a plentiful of time in analysing the data.

However, one disadvantage of using secondary data is that I would be unaware of how the data was collected, the methods that were adopted, and that would be beyond the scope, of the dissertation process.
I would also need to decide regarding to what extend the data is valid, and how to compare, and collect the data, from CSR market reports, through external press sources.

Hence, it becomes important to check the reputation of the data source, so that no distortion occurs, in the data collection through secondary research.

Therefore, it will be important to check, whether some parts of CSR reports are not mere marketing campaigns, through cross checking the information, contained through internet searches, on Google.

This can also be checked through references that the retail CSR reports have put in each chapter, or the source of the news, at the end of official retail websites. It will also help in checking the reliability of the data collected, for analysis.

When doing a search on 'Google Scholar,' regarding 'CSR in retail UK,' I tried to evaluate the methodology of the journal articles, and the similarities that matched the preparation, for the research methodology.

I concluded that the research methodology has not fully proved effective. More secondary data analysis would have provided greater scope, in the research process. Hence, the time limit and the word limit likely prove as barriers, for the process of answering my research questions, in depth.

However, the research methodology has helped in providing a positive relation of CSR activity, of the companies, and its relationships, with the stakeholders.

In supporting my research methodology, there will be a time limit set on the first research objective, that takes into consideration the carbon emission reduction, in the UK retail market industry. The time limit will be set to five years because the base year set for carbon emission reduction would be compared, and performance of supermarkets, will be drawn, through proper data evaluation. There will also be an advantage than doing primary surveys, as information gathered would lead to comprehensive, and quick conclusions.

Hence, there is a chance that higher quality data can be already available, than collecting through primary sources, when keeping UK retail, into consideration.

The second objective has been based mainly on external press sources. I will be using external sources, like websites of charitable, and philanthropic organisations, like 'British Cancer Research', 'UK Fund Raising', and internal press sources, which are available, on the website, of these retail companies, like 'Jobs Asda', 'Sainsbury's PLC', and 'Waitrose Media Centre'. An analysis will be done, on the pattern of philanthropic investment, done by these retailers, and commonality, will be identified.

The third objective is also based, on the lines of the second objective. External websites, such as 'Farming UK,' 'Ethical Green,' and CSR reports, will be investigated for the research, so that proper accreditation of supplies, and sourcing, with integrity, are investigated. Finally, a commonality will be identified.

Research Case I

Ascertaining the performance of environmental reporting by researching into carbon emission reduction, improving energy efficiency, packaging, and waste management initiatives in large UK supermarket industry, for the last five years.

Asda Ltd.

According to Asda Sustainability Report (2007), the company intended to reduce road miles by 25%, and took 4.5 million miles off the roads, to trains, in pursuit of carbon emission reductions. Trucks with automatic gearboxes saw a benefit of fuel efficiency of 1-2%, and the entire fleet of trucks claimed to save one million litres of diesel.

According to Asda Sustainability Strategy (2012), *Asda* will include the cost of carbon emission reduction, in their return of investment, and have claimed to reduce carbon footprint, by 11.9%, from 2007 to 2011.

According to Asda Carbon Footprint Report (2010), *Asda* has focused to reduce emissions, from three key areas including refrigerant gas leak reductions, energy efficiency and diverting waste from landfill. *Asda* claims of using a comprehensive programme, aimed to tackle these key areas. 100% of the food waste is claimed to be diverted from landfill, often to specialist food waste facilities, where it is often used to generate electricity. 91% of waste is claimed to be re-used or recycled. *Asda* has set a target to reduce emissions by 10%. In 2008, the carbon emission reduction has been 3.1%, followed by 4.7% in 2009, and 4.2% in 2010.

According to Freight Transport Association (2011), *Asda* has signed the Logistics Carbon Reduction Scheme, to measure, and ultimately reduce its emissions from lorries and vans. By providing fuel usage, fleet and activity data, *Asda* wants to help the logistics sector, in the UK, to paint the accurate picture, of its own carbon footprint, effectively.

As per Asda Energy & Carbon Sustainability (2012), *Asda* have claimed to develop 'low carbon bootle stores' that use 40% less energy, and emits 50% of less greenhouse gases, by using renewable energy sources, from geothermal heating, to a biomass boiler. *Asda* stores also claim to use most of the natural light, which saves around 142 tonnes of CO_2, and 349,000 kwhrs of electricity, every year. It uses sun, to produce electricity, and rain to flush the loos. There is also a 'greenroof' on stores, which is made up of grass to attract wildlife, and the stores are claimed to be landscaped, with locally sourced plants, and trees. In July 2009, *Asda* claimed to open an eco-friendly depot, which claims to be 20%, more energy efficient that uses recyclable timber and waste. The depot claims to use solar energy to power air conditioning. *Asda* have also claimed, to build new stores, which produce 60% less emissions, than stores which were set up in 2005.

According to Customer Insight (2011), a key contributor

for *Asda*, in carbon emission reduction, is the usage of eco-friendly refrigerants, that are used to preserve meat, dairy products, with a focus for energy consumption.

According to Asda Store Waste (2012), *Asda* claims to have diverted 94% of the waste of the operations, from landfill. It is also ascertained that over 95% of the construction waste is diverted from landfill. Asda Service Centres (ASC's) are claimed to be the hub of recycling efforts. The recycling points sit next to the distribution centers, and delivery trucks, claim to take all the product waste, from delivery stores to the recycling points. This approach is assumed to lower pollution, fuel efficiency, and reducing road miles, thereby contributing towards environmental sustainability, through increased CSR initiatives.

Tesco Ltd.

According to Tesco Greener Living (2012), Tesco's target is to cut CO_2 emissions, by 50%, in the UK, until 2012. *Tesco* has planned to reduce the empty lorries, on the road with partnership, with other companies. Tesco is also using double decker trailer, which carries 55 per cent, more products per journey, therefore aiming carbon emission reduction. *Tesco* has its own train system to carry goods, in some parts of the UK, which saves over 14, 560 lorry journeys', per year. Battery power vans are also in operations, which save around 180 tonnes of CO_2 every year. Seven hybrid cars in service save around 10-15 percent of fuel each year. *Tesco* also uses barges via water routes to transfer wine, slashing carbon emissions around 80 per cent.

According to Tesco CSR Report (2011), the company have claimed to save around 165,000 tonnes, of CO_2, in UK, by reducing leakage of fridge gas, which leads towards global warming effects. There was a 1% reduction in carbon emission as compared, to 2010. Low carbon stores are cutting carbon footprint, by eco-friendly designs allowing more sunlight. *Tesco* is also currently installing energy boards in UK that has an interactive award-winning touchscreen which allows staff to act where energy is used in real time. It is aimed to save 2 million pounds cost savings every year, and saving around 15,000 tonnes of CO2 emissions. It has also been claimed that *Tesco* has launched world's first 'zero carbon stores' which claims to use as much less energy as possible. The heating and cooling systems in these stores use 66% less energy than normal stores. The stores generate own energy, on site through a Combined Heat and Power (CHP) system, which uses sustainable bio-fuel from fish oil and to generate heat and power, aiming for CO2 reductions.

Therefore, excess electricity is exported to national grids in UK, increasing energy efficiency. The whole initiative is aimed to save around 2000 tonnes of CO2 every year. *Tesco* have also installed non-HFC natural refrigeration, aiming to reduce carbon emissions, by 15%, in 2012, in the UK. *Tesco* have also installed four wind turbines, in UK, using renewable energy, which is aimed to save around 3,200 tonnes, of CO2 emissions, and aiming to power 500 homes, with surplus power getting transferred to the national grid.

According to Greener Tesco (2012), *Tesco* uses automated recycling centres that easily recycle cans, glasses, and plastic bottles. The plastic waste, in turn, is used to generate energy to provide power to the national grid in UK.

According to Tesco CSR Report (2011), *Tesco* claims to be the largest recycler of cardboard, processing nearly 300,000 tonnes a year. *Tesco* also claims to recycle 22,000 tonnes of plastic every year, and provides battery recycling, for its consumers.

As a signatory of WRAP (Waste and Resources Action

Programme), an agreement has been reached to increase recycling initiatives, and grocery packaging, to lower the carbon impact by 10% till 2012.

Waitrose Ltd.

According to Waitrose CSR Report (2012), Waitrose vans are powered with biomethane gas, extracted from landfill sites. The company had set a 10-year base line, for carbon emission reduction, with 2010, as the base year, in tackling climate change. As sales grew by 10.6%, there was a 5.6% carbon emission reduction, in 2010. Waitrose also claims to participate in the Government's Carbon Reduction Commitment Scheme, by monitoring, and reporting carbon emissions, through improved carbon data, by good data quality, and granularity of the emission sources. In 2011, the emission from transport was just under 73,000 tonnes, a 5.9% improvement per million sales, since 2005/06. *Waitrose* also uses multi-deck trailers, which provide significant carbon emission reduction.

The company is planning to modify deck trailers through aerodynamic mouldings adopted from aerospace and formula one industry to optimise vehicle aerodynamics. Waitrose is also implementing vehicle telematics to assess driving styles and fuel efficiency which could save 4% of CO_2 per vehicle every year. The aim was to have telematics in every *Waitrose* vehicle till 2011.

According to Waitrose CSR Report (2011), the company is also using seven heavy vehicles fuelled by pure plant oils and electric delivery vehicles, in the quest for exploring low carbon technologies and alternative fuels, such as using food waste to generate biomethane gas. The *Waitrose* fleet has rounded corners, side skirts and low resistance tyres which are aimed at fuel efficiency. *Waitrose* is also researching other forms of biofuels in developed countries to explore alternative options for fuel efficiency. *Waitrose* is also bidding for London Congestion Charge, to qualify for a fuel discount, thereby reducing costs.

Waitrose has also put several initiatives to conserve energy use through 'Close the Door' campaign. The campaign supports automatic doors that help to reduce 50% of energy when heat is turned on, and it can cut up to 10 tonnes of CO_2 in a shop, equivalent to return flights from London to Hong Kong.

Waitrose claims to source renewable sources of energy such as wind, water power, municipal and industrial waste for energy efficiency. Electricity is also sourced from tomato suppliers at Rickmansworth store (Waitrose CSR Report, 2011).

Waitrose has also developed a low carbon propane based, water refrigeration strategy and a reduction of 20%. Waitrose is committed to replace hydrofluorocarbons

(HFC's) with natural refrigerants, and installing equipment that reduce incoming voltage, thereby reducing energy consumption.

According to Eddie Energy (2012), Waitrose is using a locally sourced woodchip biomass, to cut total emissions, by 15%, through reduction of 750 tonnes per year, from its centres through renewable, and low carbon technology.

According to Waitrose Media Centre (2012a), the company has been awarded the world's first Building Research Establishment Environmental Assessment Method (BREEAM) 'Outstanding' rating, for a retail building in Stratford, London. The building was been awarded because of its environmentally friendly, and sustainable features through water cooled, propane-based features, that reduce energy demand, by 25%. The outlet also sends unusable food waste, to an anaerobic digestion plant, which manufactures renewable energy, and goes back to the national grid.

According to John Lewis (2012a), *Waitrose* was presented with 'Environmental Collaboration of the Year Award' in 2011, for its leak reduction project. In 2010, Waitrose claimed to exceed its energy efficiency target, by 20%. Waitrose has also claimed to reduce refrigerants, and cooling emissions by 50%, till 2012, compared to 2008 levels.

The company also claims to realise the importance of biodiversity, to conserve, and enhance the natural environment, near and inside its outlets. *Waitrose* outlet in Bond Way, has a living wall to promote wildlife movement, around the site, hedges, instead of conventional fencing, and nest boxes, for bats and swifts.

The whole initiative will likely help to reduce carbon dioxide emissions, around 80 per cent (Waitrose Media Centre, 2012b).

According to Food & Grocery Experts (2009), Waitrose helps to reduce food waste through careful ordering and ensuring any food waste produced is diverted into landfill. *Waitrose* is also working with farmers to reduce food waste through collaborative supply chain efforts.

According to John Lewis (2012b), *Waitrose* converts food waste, into heat and nutrient fertilisers, and recycles materials, such as plastic and cardboards. Office paper, plastic cups, toner cartridges, glass, magazines, cans, batteries, and bottles are also recycled.

Waitrose along with John Lewis partnership has set targets, to recycle 75% of waste, by 2012.

Sainsbury's Ltd.

According to J Sainbury PLC (2012), the company has claimed to achieve a direct carbon emission reduction, of 18,933 tonnes in 2011, as compared to 2010. Sainsbury's has also developed a carbon foot printing tool, specially designed for farmers which has achieved a PAS2050 standard, Tier 3 by Carbon Trust. It involves sight visits to farms, and gathering of data, rather than desk modelling exercises, in carbon emission reduction planning, to ensure data is meaningful and accurate. It has resulted in a 10 per cent reduction, in carbon emissions annually. Sustainability initiative for farmers has been directly linked towards carbon footprint reduction (Sainsbury's CSR Report, 2011).

Sainsbury's also claims to use an award-winning geothermal technology, to supply 30 per cent of its energy from renewable sources. The company also uses a Smart Grid system, in collaboration with Imperial College London, that monitors the National Grid, and activates biofuel generator, when there is increased demand for electricity. Wood chips are used to heat biomass boilers, since 2008, to heat the store, rather than fossil fuel gases. Consents are made with suppliers, to make products, which release less carbon emissions. The company also claims to persuade customers, to reduce environmental footprint (J Sainsbury PLC, 2012)

According to Clean Power Air (2012), Sainsbury's is using a Clean Air Power Genesis Dual Fuel Technology, for heavy duty diesel engines, by using a combination of diesel, and biomethane, obtained from landfill sites. The technology helps to substitute up to 80% of diesel, depending upon conditions and operating required. This initiative has been marketed as 'Running on Rubbish' programme. It makes diesel run as a spark plug. This innovation has helped in significant fuel cost savings, thereby helping in a marked reduction, in carbon emissions. This technology is claimed to have a potential to save upto 60 metric tonnes of CO_2 per year, an equivalent of 4% of UK's total carbon emission reductions. Sainsbury's also started a collaboration, with

British Gas, from February, 2011, by providing energy solutions, to customers, through lowering of bills, and energy use, by energy efficient solutions, and value for money.

According to Sainsbury's CSR Report (2011), the company has set a target of 25% carbon emission reduction, by 2012, as compared to 2006 base lines. The company also works in compliance with the Carbon Reduction Commitment Energy Efficiency Scheme. The 'Carbon Step Change' programme has implemented low- carbon innovations, in new stores, for future emission reductions.

As per J Sainsbury's PLC (2011), the company believes in a positive waste usage, by diverting all the landfill towards anaerobic digestion. It also offers light bulb recycling, at every store, along with general recycling facilities. Sainsbury's claims to run UK's first mobile handset charger recycling initiative, and have also offered customers plastic bag recycling initiatives.

Sainsbury's also claims to recycle 9,500 tonnes of plastic film, and over 140,000 tonnes of cardboard. Sainsbury also closely works with WRAP (Waste and Resources Action Programme).

The company is also giving 'nectar points' to customers on reusing a bag. Sainsbury's also claims to have removed 7% of packaging, from their own branded products, through new packaging, and design, and that has resulted in 11% package reduction. Sainsbury's has introduced heat seal lids, on soft fruit lines, removing of cartons from Tuna fillets, and reducing the size of cardboard, on pizza base mix. The whole initiative has resulted in a reduction of 87% of packaging, every year (Sainsbury's CSR Report, 2011).

A Comparative Analysis

The findings of each company likely ascertain that a

CSR strategy, for reducing carbon emissions, through transport and energy efficiency, waste management, and packaging initiatives, are been seriously taken, by the large supermarket industry, in UK.

Most of the CSR initiative regarding carbon emission reduction, improved packaging, increased energy efficiency, and waste management seem to be converging. Several innovations in technology, are helping these companies, to attain leverages, in environmental sustainability.

In the quest for environmental sustainability, the companies have put forward initiatives for alternative fuels, usage of natural refrigerants, which signify the importance of research and development, for competitive advantages, in the large retail sector of the UK. The need for environmental sustainability in UK retail industry, through CSR has likely allowed companies in enhancing their societal concerns, and as well enhancing their reputation, through environmental awareness.

Asda Ltd. is relying on introducing automatic gearboxes, while *Waitrose* is planning to implement new designs of trucks, to reduce emissions, and innovative tyres. *Tesco*, on the other hand, is planning to reduce its trucks on the roads, in collaboration with other companies. Battery and hybrid cars, are also being introduced by *Tesco*, which seems as an effective strategy than others. However, *Waitrose* and *Sainsbury's* have realised the need of effectively collaborating with suppliers, in reducing carbon emissions, unlike *Asda* and *Tesco*.

Sainsbury's is introducing a superior technology of fuel in its trucks that might attain significant reductions in CO_2 emissions, through a combination of biomethane gas and diesel, which might act as a competitive advantage, for the company in the future, unlike other companies.

On the other hand, an interesting initiative of *Tesco*, which may likely act beneficial for its CSR promotion, is finding a substitute in trains and water transport, through easing off good transport, through roads. This initiative will likely reduce tonnes of carbon emission, in the UK large supermarket industry.

All four supermarkets namely *Tesco, Waitrose, Asda, and Sainsbury's* are planning to introduce environmentally friendly stores, in the future. However, Asda claims that the design of its futuristic eco-friendly stores use maximum solar energy, while *Tesco* claims to use an award-winning touch board in its stores, which prompts the employees to act, regarding energy efficiency. *Waitrose* also has been introducing award winning eco-friendly stores. These initiatives also suggest a need for eco-friendly designs of stores, for the success of CSR initiatives. These initiatives also indicate the visions for responsible business, in the future of retail, in United Kingdom.

In UK, several awards and affiliating up with carbon reduction schemes, likely act as motivators, and suggest the need for awarding companies, which thrive to increase societal concerns, through their business strategies.

Waitrose has been awarded, for its performance, in curbing refrigerant leakages, by Carbon Trust Standard, while *Sainsbury's* have been accredited by Carbon Trust, for its innovative carbon foot printing tool. *Asda* and *Waitrose* have joined Government's Carbon Reduction Scheme, which also justifies the role of legislation, in dealing with the initiatives of carbon emissions, signifying the need of environmental sustainability laws, at upper administrative, or governmental levels.

In achieving CSR, all the four supermarkets have set targets through base years, regarding carbon emission reduction, and are improving through achieving increased performance, through sustained low emissions.

A need to divert all the landfill to productive energy efficiency, the introduction of biomass boilers, and usage of woodchips, is helping to achieve self- dependence, in energy generation, and using less energy, from non-renewable sources, such as electricity, from the national grid. *Sainsbury's*, however, have a computer managed system, which gets activated, whenever energy is needed, from biomass boilers, unlike other three companies.

Therefore, the less quest for relying on non-renewable sources of energy is likely helpful, in attaining successful CSR initiatives, through energy efficiency.

All the four companies have packaging and waste management initiatives, in order. All four companies claim to recycle maximum junk, rather than diverting it to land fill. However, *Tesco* has been the first retailer to start automatic battery recycling points, unlike other three companies, while as Sainsbury's claims to modify packaging design, for package reduction, thereby reducing waste. Sainsbury also works also with WRAP (Waste and Resource Action Programme) initiative, signifying the need for social campaigns in the quest for better waste management.

Waitrose, on the other hand, is more focused of achieving higher targets, in waste management. *Asda*, however, has developed waste management centres, nearby its distribution, and the company claims that it not only diverts waste, but also realises fuel efficiency, and less carbon emissions, at the same time. The plan denotes the importance of proximity, in running operations for competitiveness. *Asda* also claims to convert food waste, into electricity.

Therefore, there is a difference, in approach, in attaining positive waste management initiatives, but the core strategy to implement environmental ethics, through

CSR, has been imperative, for all four large retailers, in UK

Research Case II

Determining how the supermarket industry in the UK applies sustainable policies of corporate philanthropy through local community development

Asda Ltd.

According to Breast Cancer Campaign (2012), *Asda* has raised over £29 billion for Breast Cancer Care through sales of pink products, and in store fundraising, with Asda colleagues, and customers through 'Asda's Tickled Pink Campaign'. It has resulted to help fund 78 research projects, in 20 locations, and supported six scientific fellowships, worth over £3 million. The charity has also helped in creating a vital resource, for breast cancer, for researchers, in UK and Ireland.

Asda has also raised £943,880.45 for Tommy's, helping to ensure that fewer babies die, during pregnancy, or birth. It has ensured that no family is alone for health measures, during pregnancy complications (Asda Charities, 2012a).

According to Asda Charities (2012b), *Asda* donated £20,000 to complete the construction of a roof, at Throstle Nest Riding School. It was done so that the arena would allow lessons in cold or wet weather. It has allowed smooth functioning, of a long running RDA (Riding for the Disabled Association), in Pudsey, West Yorkshire.

According to Asda Charities (2012c), *Asda* raised a £1.5 million for 'BBC Children in Need' through regular fundraising events, and activities, around the store, within local communities, at different, places across UK.

As per Everyman (2012), *Asda* has helped the organisation, by raising and donating around £600k, for research, into prostrate and testicular cancer, in the year 2011. Asda helped through promoting Everyman products, and holding car boot sales, to charity football matches, to raise awareness, for charity, and involving customers.

According to Asda Charities (2012d), *Asda* is supporting the 'Pedal Power Campaign', and has raised over '£1.2 million to help children, and youth in Scotland, Wales, and Northern Ireland, between the ages 10 and 20.

As per Bike Club (2012), the funding will allow the groups to buy new bikes, and safety equipment, for their cycling project, to encourage more young people, to cycle.

According to Jobs Asda (2012), *Asda* foundation has donated £13,000 to a drop-in centre, in Glasgow, for Children's charity 'With Kids'. It is transformed into a fully equipped centre, providing support, to some 350 disadvantaged children, and families. In 2011 August street riots, *Asda* helped the people of Tottenham, by donating food, clothing, and housing goods. *Asda* is also providing job opportunities, such as work placements in finance and pharmacy, to local communities, wherever the stores are operational.

Tesco Ltd.

According to Tesco CSR Report (2011), *Tesco* has contributed over £10 million, raised by staff for charities, and good causes. *Tesco* believes that their stores are central for any community engagement. *Tesco* started philanthropic fairs in 2009, and increased them from 20 to 100 in 2010. The fairs took place featuring a combination of stalls. *Tesco* also opened six 'Regeneration Partnership' stores, in the UK, and created atleast 600 jobs, for long term unemployed people. About 90% of the *Tesco* Staff are satisfied, regarding pension, which they regard as an important influence, on how they stay, with the business.

According to Tesco Charity Trust (2012), about £700,000 community award donations, were made into charities.

Tesco charities aim to support at a local level, to support the needs of employees, customers, and communities around the stores.

As per UK fundraising (2012a), *Tesco* staff raised £10.5 million, during its Charity of the Year partnership, with Alzhemier's Society, and Alzhemier Scotland. The partnership involved 4,157 fundraising events, with 550 members of staff, taking on these challenges.

According to Cancer Research UK (2012a), *Tesco* raised over £10 million to help beat cancer, through early diagnosis, and detection. There will be a national three-day collection, in October, where Tesco will raise £50,000 through customer philanthropy. *Tesco* is also collecting electrical goods, to benefit Cancer Research, by encouraging shoppers, to donate used electrical items, so that the company can recycle them, for Cancer Research UK (Cancer Research UK, 2012b).

According to Civil Society Fundraising (2011), *Tesco* is raising money for women's health charities, through feminine products. It has launched a 'Halo Initiative' that supports organisations, in the UK, and Republic of Ireland, whose main work include fighting ovarian, and breast cancer, and helping women, with mental health issues, and protecting women from domestic violence.

Tesco also raised £7.2m for Clic Sargent, as part of its 2010 'charity of the year partnership'.

Waitrose

According to Waitrose CSR report (2011), John Lewis, which owns *Waitrose*, introduced the initiative 'Charity of the Year, 2010', for beating bowel cancer. It was benefitted by various fundraising activities, such as mobile recycling scheme, which gave donation, for every phone received.

In 2011, *Waitrose* donated £2.7m to 8,500 to causes in

the local communities, wherever stores are operational. In 2011, *Waitrose* sponsored the Royal Horticultural Society's Campaign for School Gardening, which aims to have 80% of the UK's 21,500 primary schools, using a garden, by the end of 2012. It is stated that through wages, *Waitrose* contributes £1.7m to the local economy. The company is also supporting Music to support social causes to enhance human lives.

According to John Lewis Partnership (2012), *Waitrose* community matters donated over £3m to local causes. *Waitrose* also works as a 'partnership,' so that the shops become part of the communities, they are based in. When making new stores, *Waitrose* tries to initiate community involvement, so that it suits the surroundings, and long-term value. *Waitrose* has also tried to initiative job opportunities, outside its staff membership, for unemployed, in regeneration, and growth of the UK economy.

As per CTS Retail (2012), Waitrose has committed to donate surplus food, from all its retail branches, to UK Charities, by the end of 2012.

According to UK Fundraising (2012b), Community Matters has operated, in Waitrose's branch stores, for some time. Every month all Waitrose branches donate online a sum of £1,000 (£500 in Convenience Shops), to be shared by three local good causes. *Waitrose* also voted for one of three national charities, to receive a share of a 25,000 donation, after three months.

According to Variety (2012), each month throughout June, July and August, Variety, the Children's Charity, will be one of the three national charities, to receive a share of £25,000, through the Waitrose Community Matters scheme.

As per Alzhemier's Society (2012), Waitrose Community

Matters has chosen to tackle Alzhemier's disease, and further donated £25,000. John Lewis, which has an affiliation with *Waitrose*, has donated 23,790 hours of staff to charity work, during 2010. It is the highest number of working hours devoted, since the scheme began, ten years ago.

According to Asthma UK (2012), the company has been selected as the beneficiary of Waitrose community matters online scheme.

Waitrose has also planned to launch a partner volunteering scheme, which will oversee that all 277 of its branches donate 250 hours of employee's time to local charities, and good causes, each year (Waitrose Media Centre, 2012d).

According to Nidderdale team (2012), Nidderdale AONB (Area of Outstanding Beauty), situated in Yorkshire, has been nominated for the worthy causes of *Waitrose*.

Sainsbury's

According to RNIB (2012), a local charity is planned to get sponsored, by the organisation, called RNIB 'Sunshine High School', as South Ruslip for 2012/2013. The organisation provides a supportive environment, for blind and partially sighted children. *Sainsbury's* will support it for twelve months.

According to Home Start (2012), the organisation has been chosen as the local charities of the year. *Sainsbury's* will help the customers to continue their essential family work, so that they may be able to recruit new volunteers.

According to J Sainsbury's PLC (2012), the company launched its first ever food drive, the One Million Meal Appeal with the charity partner, Fare Share. Following the event, the food was sent to 17 depots across the country, and being distributed to 700 charities served by Fareshare daily.

According to Sainsbury's Castlepoint Charity Donation (2012), Sainsbury's have nominated a generous cheque of £2020. Sainsbury's also have donated to Beverly Primary School, and donated £700 pounds (HU 17, 2012).

According to Inside Games (2012), *Sainsbury's* also has helped to raise more than £100m for school sports, since its launch of the Active Kids scheme, in 2005.

The company believes that it is the largest ever donation, to youth groups, and kids. It has given a chance to children, to be more active, in their daily lives. The company provided among 141,739 rainbow skipping ropes, 71,143 foam Javelins, and 37,810 Mitre Tactic footballs. It has been claimed, by the firm, that it is the biggest donation ever, by any UK retailer.

According to Rutland & Stamford Mercury (2012), Sainsbury's donated over £200, to the friends of Bourne Wood. The donation will go towards trees, stakes, wires, and ties.

A Comparative Analysis

The findings ascertain that *Asda* has donated to causes related to health and fitness philanthropy, while as *Tesco* is converging with Asda's corporate philanthropy mission, of mainly focussing on charitable causes, regarding cancer causes, but *Tesco* has also stressed on community development, especially on feminine product sponsorship. The striking feature of *Tesco's* policy is community development, being central to its mission.

Waitrose, on the other hand, has devoted initiatives, for beating bowel cancer, and fighting Alzheimer's disease.

The striking feature of Waitrose philanthropy is that it is also aiming to promote school gardening.

Sainsbury's has been donating food and helping blind children.

However, the important feature of Sainsbury's is that it is supporting school kids, for extra circular activities, and giving donation, towards garden development. The aim is to serve the CSR mission, at local community levels.
Therefore, the philanthropic causes, from UK retail sector, are mainly aimed for enhancement of health, fighting diseases, and donating food, mainly aimed for societal and economical upliftment, in the United Kingdom.

Research Case III

Enquiring into responsible sourcing of food products in UK CSR industry which are traded through ethical farming standards.

Asda Ltd.

According to Farming UK (2007), Asda's ethical food sourcing policy runs into 260 stores, all over England, Wales, and Scotland.

It has also prompted much interest amongst local farmers, in company's food sourcing policy. *Asda* is also supporting a localisation drive, to produce and harvest socially responsible food.

Local sourcing through ethical standards will keep proper consideration of pesticides, fertiliser, and fresher produce (Retail Week, 2007).

Asda is also trying to establish Asda Farm Link schemes (partnership groups with suppliers) for milk, beef, lamb, and pork. This initiative has helped to propagate ethical farming links, to improve livelihood, and health of consumers.

Asda has also invested £99m in perishable supply chain, by the end of 2015. It means that the customers will likely get the highest quality fresh food.

Asda has also claimed to run several research and development programmes, for beef, poultry, pork, lamb, and diary produce, by the end of 2015.

Independent consultants are also employed, to support Asda's daily farming practices.

Some of the sustainable food partnerships, which *Asda* wants to employ, in running the CSR initiative, for the retail supermarkets is ethical sourcing of palm oil, developing a sustainable beef programme, and selling sustainable fish. For this initiative, *Asda* has opened two new Agricultural Colleges, and joined Sustainable Fish Partnerships, to independently verify achievements (Parliament UK, 2012).

Asda is also trying to work with certain certification bodies, such as Soil Association, to increase the number of organic products, on offer to our consumers.

Asda has also developed initiatives, for finding ways, to improve cattle welfare, to follow an ethical sourcing programme (Asda Sustainability, 2012).

Asda Ltd. has also aimed to produce healthy food,

by promoting food, by displaying a certain number or products, which means the minimum government standards, as set by UKROFS. For example, *Asda* is trying its best to manufacture best quality locally produced cheese (First Milk, 2012). Cumbrian seafood, on the other hand, has started to supply *Asda*, with responsibly sourced lemon sole fillets.

The company uses boats with proven responsible 'seine net' method that does not destroy the seabed, and minimises the number of juvenile fish caught.

Therefore, for ethical sourcing standards, through collaboration, with reputable suppliers has proven beneficial for *Asda* (Fish Site, 2009).

Asda had also taken Brazilian beef off its shelves, due to the reason that it could have originated, from farms, with foot and mouth diseases. Therefore, to sustain ethical sourcing standards, the company now strongly relies on high quality locally sourced beef, as 80 per cent comes, from UK (Procurement Leaders, 2012).

Asda have also produced a sustainable soil guide, in collaboration with LEAF that gives farmers advice on soil texture, drainage, compaction, nutrients and biological health. This initiative would enhance the health and stability of the soil, thereby gives rise to ethical farming standards (Aisle Asda, 2011)

Tesco Ltd.

T*esco* has initiated a plan for managing the environment. It has been reviewing the use of pesticides, considering the best prevailing agricultural practices.

The company has been working with independent agricultural experts. The company has also collaborated with Nature's Choice scheme.

This is the integrated farm management scheme. About 80% have integrated all suppliers, to the UK (Tesco Magazine, 2012).

According to Tesco Real Food (2012a), *Tesco* has organised a dedicated agricultural team, who are responsible for writing and implementing 'Livestock Codes of Practice'.

This helps the company, in all aspects of the farming, such as animal welfare, and food safety.

The agricultural team is also helping experts, to improve standards, and communication, throughout the supply chain, as well as developing products, and systems.

Tesco's beef standards are national farm insurance approved, and belong to reputable suppliers of 'Producer Clubs'. The cattle are allowed to live in well-furnished barns, till they are ready for sale (Tesco Real Food, 2012b).

The eggs at *Tesco* are audited, to check whether livestock standards are followed.

Illegal eggs are discontinued, and hens are reared, in enriched cages, due to certain legislation changes. The British Lion Code independently audits all these farms, to ensure that everything is according to standards (Tesco Real Food, 2012c).

The chicken in *Tesco* farms is reared, in barns, which provide enough sunlight, and it covers the whole life cycle, from breeding birds, through grower farms. The organic chicken is audited by one of the organic farm accreditation bodies, such as Soil Association or Organic Farmers. The birds are fed certified cereals, and are reared on atleast 70 days, which has contributed to a tasty flavour (Tesco Real Food, 2012d).

Waitrose

Waitrose is trying to implement responsible farming practices, through being an active member of LEAF (Linking Farming and Environment), which aims to combine the best of traditional farming methods, such as using modern technology, so that farmers can manage their farms, in an informed, professional, and caring way.

Waitrose is committed to promote integrated farm management schemes, to market ethical farming practices, to the consumers.

Waitrose is also trying to blend the biodiversity concerns, in such a way, that flora and fauna coexist, on the land.

This has in turn reduced the need for using chemicals. *Waitrose* is also implementing other environmental initiatives, such as tree and hedge planting, arable margins, as well as pasture and grassland management (Waitrose Media Centre, 2012d).

According to Waitrose CSR Report (2004), Waitrose sources its fruit, and vegetable produce, from technologies, such as ICM'S, which ensure best horticultural practices, site selection, and husbandry.

The company also uses Hazard Analysis and Critical Point Systems, that is used in food production, to identify specific hazards, and measures, for their control.

It also provides risk assessment required by hygiene regulations. Fish, which are sold in Waitrose, are accredited by Marine Stewardship Council, for sustainable, and well managed fisheries.

Waitrose is also developing research, into livestock genetics. for healthier animals, efficient, and better environment, to reap the benefits of ethical farming, in CSR retail industry.

The company is also protecting farmers, for long term supply relationships, to preserve the fragile economy. It is also ensuring that high quality food is sourced, so that it strengthens the link, between farmers and consumers.

LEAF (Linking Environment and Farming) initiative is also helping *Waitrose* to promote ethically right practices, to protect the farms, in the UK country side, by adhering to the series of Integrated Farm Management principles, including efficient soil management techniques, the use of crop cultivation, careful choice of seed varieties, a commitment to animal welfare, wildlife habitats, and management of landscape, and rural communities (Waitrose Inspiration, 2012).

Sainsbury's

Sourcing at Sainsbury's means taking different considerations into account, such as working in partnership, with our suppliers, supporting British farmers, promoting animal welfare, supporting fair trade, and sustainable sourcing.

The company is also committed to organic methods of farming (J Sainsbury PLC, 2012).

According to Ethical and Green (2012), Sainsbury's have set corporate responsibility, for ethical sourcing, namely 'sourcing with integrity'.

The company is also launching a farming initiative, where it wants more locally sourced, and high-quality organic apples (Ethical and Green, 2012).

The company is also boosting sustainability, through making stronger supply chains.

Over £1 billion are being invested, to provide significant opportunities, for ethical farming, in the British Food Industry.

Sainsbury's have claimed to make revolutionary steps, in animal welfare, such as indoor free farming trial, at the concept farm, in Yorkshire.

The company is also committed to sell British Lamb, which is best of seasons. For raising ethical sourcing standards, local farmers are recruited, who have familiar knowledge, of the management of farms. It has claimed to source all whole eggs, from cage free hens.

The company has also won a prestigious award, from compassion in World Farming, at Good Farm Animal Welfare Awards. *Sainsbury's* is persuading farmers, to apply sustainable way, including best calf recommendation, Good Diary category (J Sainsburys PLC, 2012d).

Sainsbury's sources Scottish farmed Atlantic with the farmer supplier, Marine Harvest, as a sustainable aquaculture (J Sainsbury's PLC, 2012e).

The company also claims to be the first British market, to

stock British Fish Fingers, using ethically sourced palm oil, certified from certified Roundtable, on Sustainable Palm Oil (RSPO) sources.

In 2010, 93 per cent of the wood, used for Sainsbury's products, was made from Forest Stewardship Council (FSC), or recycled sources.

Over 12 per cent of the company's own sources are independently certified ethically sourced sources, such as Marine Stewardship Council, Fair trade, and Freedom Foods.
For raising ethical sourcing standards, the company has developed a sustainability rating system, for wild caught fish, with input from the supply base, environmental organisations, and fishery scientists.

All branded farmed salmon is sourced from RSPCA Freedom food welfare standards, from Scottish salmon farms (Sainsbury's 20 by 20 Sustainability Plan, 2010).

A Comparative Analysis

There have been different approaches, to ethical farming practices, by four retail companies.

The striking feature of *Asda* is that they have put faith, in educative measures, so that it benefits the consumers, in a healthy manner, by starting colleges, and doing soil research.

Tesco, on the other hand, have been implementing a 'code of conduct' that ensure ethical farming practices, are conducted, without any evasions, from fundamental ethics, that companies believe in carrying the farming practices. *Tesco* has also taken steps for animal welfare, unlike *Asda*.

Tesco have been following a different approach. They believe that only accreditations can ensure that ethical trading practices are reaching the consumers through sourcing products with integrity.

Waitrose, on the other hand, have been using technological measures, for enhancing farming standards, in an ethical way, like integrated farm management, and hazard analysis, that have been used as disaster management tools, by *Waitrose*, to protect ethical farming standards, that has been unique to *Waitrose*.
Sainsbury's have laid stress, on improving supply chains, to improve ethical farming standards. The other striking feature has been taking steps, to improve animal welfare.

Conclusion

CSR, in United Kingdom, has been implemented, due to the realisation of the fact that social responsibility carries outmost importance, in doing business. Companies namely *Asda, Sainsbury's, Waitrose,* and *Tesco* have been trying to do business with integrity, so that they market a sustainable approach, in doing business.

Therefore, it can be said that the companies are trying to sell their ethical way of doing business, to consumers, to enhance the reputational value of their business.

The environmental concern, of the retail sector, has been an important aspect, to consider, for implementing CSR, because it also convergences with governmental policies, of the UK legislation.

Retail sector is also trying several technological measures, and architectural restructuring, in helping to integrate environmental concerns, and their protection. All the mentioned retail companies, in the UK, are trying to implement carbon emission reduction, through technological improvements.

Therefore, the research has strongly proved that for initiating environmental sustainability programmes, innovation through technology will not only help in achieving business goals, but will also fulfil the objectives, of the local government.

The UK retail sector, overall, has also made revolutionary steps, in improving the health standards of people, around UK.

Hence, it can be said that the CSR in UK retail sector has proved as a good corporate citizenship initiative and certain British ideals continue to shape the foundations of Corporate Social Responsibility.

The process of carbon emission reductions has resulted as a mark of excellence, in taking real action, on climate change, in United Kingdom. The goal of CSR is likely providing health benefits, so that businesses through retail sector, result in high moral behavioural attitudes, to flourish the competitive conditions, of the third millennium.

This whole initiative of CSR, in the UK retail industry, has blended very well with the corporate regulations, that have been drafted into the business models, of the respective retailers.

The result, of the research, has likely resulted that business companies namely *Asda*, *Sainsbury's*, *Tesco* and *Waitrose*, have been trying to act under the spirit of law, and ethical standards.

The research shows that the Corporate Social Responsibility, in retail, provides a visionary scope, for the betterment of society, and its performance depends upon the nature of the enterprise, and the stakeholder impacts. This likely holds true when CSR works, as corporate philanthropy, through charity and volunteering. It has likely resulted, in a revolutionary change, in the functioning of retail businesses, all over UK.

Therefore, it is through the idea of socially responsible investment, for the creation of value, companies in the UK retail have been initiating CSR programmes, for the upliftment of social, and environmental standards.

By reduction of emissions through technology, construction of environmentally friendly buildings, corporate philanthropy through local community investments, and increase of ethical farming standards, through sourcing with integrity, and strengthening the local supply chain, retail companies in the UK, are providing new ways to tap competitive advantages, for company strategy.

These CSR initiatives, such as community investments, have resulted in mutual economic development, and creation of jobs, for the communities. The research has found out that corporate mission, and business ethics, play a pivotal role, in the creation of corporate social responsibility.

The awareness of a moral responsibility, is the only way, through which societal upliftment can be made.

The findings can be concluded in saying that CSR, in the UK retail sector, has resulted as a way for the companies, to sustain, in the competitive market, through initiatives, which look achievable, by the company. It has provided the companies a way to maximise the profits.

CSR initiatives, through strong advocacy, have provided ways, for the vision of sustainable growth, in the UK retail market.

The findings also suggest that retail companies, in the UK, are becoming socially responsible, because stakeholders understand, and address the local community issues, that are relevant to them.

The research further concludes that CSR initiatives are positively accepted, only if they are at the interests of shareholders, and do not have a detrimental impact, on the organisation.

Managerial decisions, which are taken for CSR initiatives, have likely resulted as business benefits, that can be derived from increased employee engagement.

This has likely indicated that companies should act as responsible entities, otherwise it will have repercussions, from the society.

The dissertation has also provided an argument, regarding market forces, that can be directly linked to economic functions, through which CSR initiatives operate.

It can be, hence, concluded, that the CSR initiatives are helping retail market forces, in UK, to act in a socially responsible way.

Personal Reflections

Writing a dissertation for a master's degree is always challenging. In fact, my previous bachelor's degree in commerce had no research content, for pursuing a dissertation coursework. Therefore, having enthusiasm, for pursuing a postgraduate dissertation research, I still had no idea how to go through.

Firstly, I invested a long of time to think about the type of research I wanted to do. I was initially thinking to pursue a dissertation regarding motivational traits, in management, for a small company.

However, the risks of getting access to a management company, and not having much specialised knowledge, in psychology, and uncertainty of writing an extensive thesis, about motivation in management, without highly recommended primary research, under competitive time constraints, made me rethink about the idea.

It was also for this reason that I was unsure, whether I could successfully critique its relevant literature theories.

Amidst the first semester itself, I was trying to jot down some research objectives, and a dissertation topic, regarding motivation in management, but I was somehow unsatisfied, about the outcome.

I chose Corporate Social Responsibility as a dissertation topic, because I was influenced, by the idea of social responsibility, in business. It had its origins in Europe, especially Great Britain.

I also used to follow daily happenings, regarding the topic, and once commented upon CSR initiatives, of Tata Sons Ltd., at my college, in my home place in Kashmir, where our 'business club' debates happened.

I was very confident of doing a good quality literature review, about the topic, and was also optimistic blending personal opinions, and critical analysis.

The research for my dissertation was extensive. I tried to search journal articles, through Google Scholar, and searched websites, like Business in the Community, Food and Grocery Experts, CSR Europe, and CSR news, to get necessary updates, to inform myself, regarding the position of Corporate Social Responsibility, as a movement, in Europe.

I was very much-impressed by the way different business leaders, or even governments, for that matter of fact, had included sustainability programmes in their decisions, to have positive social impacts, in the society.

My research objective making process was getting prepared around mid-January 2012. After its conclusion, the objectives looked satisfactory to me.

However, after discussions with my supervisor, I began to realise that I needed to certain amendments, regarding the dissertation title, and research objectives.

My supervisor helped me understand the need for SMART research objectives, that would promote the basis of a successful master's dissertation.

The classes regarding postgraduate research methodology, also helped me, to learn how to structure, organise time, and importance of original research, for a master's thesis.

As topics are chosen, and developed by students themselves, in postgraduate level dissertation studies, the creation of a suitable dissertation felt very necessary.

The title of my dissertation in the research was:

A study on Corporate Social Responsibility (CSR) as a responsive strategy to enhance competitive advantage through sustainability in business.

The research objectives drafted in the proposal were:

-To examine the evolution of CSR in business strategy

-To ascertain the ways of sustainability by researching into the business plans of leading companies in the retail sector

-To determine the basis of CSR driven innovation in business strategies

After discussions with my supervisor, and the personal reflection, necessary to carry out the development of objectives, I thought that my dissertation title was too descriptive, and too broad, in scope, to carry out a dissertation process, for a master's thesis.

I began to think that CSR in UK retail would be a nice idea, for development, as I came to a certain conclusion, after further review of retail websites, and CSR reports, from the official websites because there was some kind of originality about them. It took me around ten days, to do the initial reviewing process, before the submission of ethics form, in March.

After more was analysis done, the first objective historically seemed descriptive to me, which I would have used, in the introduction, of my dissertation.

However, I also started to realise that I could research about technological advancements, namely CSR driven innovation, in business strategies, in the retail sector itself.

I already wanted to research about ethical sourcing in supermarkets.

Hence, I decided to research about CSR, in UK supermarkets, with particular emphasis, for the development of research objectives.

I then started to write on the research objectives, so that there is some kind of originality, and capability of developing objectives, for a master's dissertation.

Hence the amendment of my dissertation title was changed to:

To investigate CSR (Corporate Social Responsibility) in large supermarket industry of United Kingdom namely Asda, Tesco, Waitrose, and Sainsbury's

The amendment of my research objectives was changed to:

-To ascertain the performance of environmental reporting by researching into carbon emission reduction, improving energy use, packaging, and waste management initiatives in the last five years.

-To determine how the supermarket industry in the UK applies sustainable policies through local community development.

-To inquire into responsible sourcing of food products

which are traded through ethical farming standards.

- To evaluate how the UK supermarket industry spreads community awareness of health and diet advice through educative strategies.

The fourth outcome could not get completed due to the word limit.

I tried to construct objectives that were not too vague, and could get developed.

I also managed to get a consent letter from *Asda*. I had plans to distribute questionnaires, and to conduct interviews, for my second objective, before the amendment.

However, I then realised that it was better to have objectives that could have a secondary research methodology only, as my findings and research would likely become complicated.

The amendment to my research objectives completely changed my perceptions, of doing primary research, in the dissertation process.

Also, I started to realise that it was against the time constraints, to develop findings, through primary research, and then have a comparative analysis.
The other reason is that the sample size would have not been significant, and the conclusions would have been elusive.

A lot of motivation and hard work was required, to complete the dissertation process. Sometimes, long hours were required at a stretch, especially during the night.

Therefore, planning was very necessary, especially when it came to writing research objectives.

I had to make sure that the data is collected, in a logically coherent way, using relevant sources. I also had to make sure that referencing was done, in the recommended way.

It also took me some time to think about the structuring, and writing the research methodology.

I had to carefully think about the pros and cons, of both qualitative and quantitative analysis, while writing the research methodology.

The ability to take direction mattered a lot during the dissertation process. Goal setting was also very important, and I followed that according to the instructions of the supervisor.

I also began to learn that the whole idea of dissertation was to develop critical thinking, content analysis, and skills that form the heart of the work.

The other important thing, which a researcher learns, is that several skills are transferred into a career.

Many opportunities are in prospects during the job recruitments.

CSR professionals have extensive knowledge about societal obligations, in business, and many modern MNC's (multinational companies) have felt the need for CSR professionals, in their companies, because of the environmental concerns, and philanthropic initiatives.

Having learnt extensively about CSR, through reading literature, its critical analysis, and opinion, I am very hopeful that I will likely gain a job in CSR sector, especially in supermarkets, where I have learnt how companies implement, ethical sourcing, after my researching process. I have learnt many transferable skills, while pursuing the dissertation in CSR retail. It includes how companies can acquire a moral responsibility in business, in understanding the relationship between business and society.

The skills of a CSR consultant, are thus transferred, towards decisions on environmental sustainability, by applying technological improvements.

I am confident about debating and implementing CSR initiatives, whenever I get a chance, to discourse on managerial matters.

References

1. Aisle Asda (2012) 'Asda and LEAF combine to launch Sustainable Soils Guide' [Available at: http://your.asda.com/aislespy-sustainable-sourcing/asda-and-leaf-launch-sustainable-soils-guide, Accessed: 13th August, 2012]

2. Asda Charities (2012a) 'Asda helps to save babies lives over the phone' [Available at: http://charities.asda.com/2011/12/30/helping-to-save-babies-lives-over-the-phone, Accessed: 7th June, 2012]

3. Asda Charities (2012b) 'Asda raises the roof at Throstle Nest Riding School' [Available at: http://charities.asda.com/2011/12/4/we-raise-the-roof-at-throstle-nest-riding-school, Accessed: 7th June, 2012]

4. Asda Charities (2012c) 'Asda raises money for children in need' Available at: http://charities.asda.com/2010/11/22/a-great-result-asda-raises-1-5million-for-bbc-children-in-need, Accessed: 8th June, 2012]

5. Asda Charities (2012d) 'More kids on their bikes – thanks to Pedal Power 2009' Available: http://charities.asda.com/charities-bike-club, Accessed: 8th June, 2012]

6. Asda Energy & Carbon Sustainability (2012) ' We are switching off and cutting back' [Available at: http://your.asda.com/sustainability-energy, Accessed: 20th May, 2012]

7. Asda Sustainability Strategy (2012) ' Asda Environmental Sustainability Targets' [Available at: http://your.asda.com/system/dragonfly/production/2012/02/28/09_37_08_670_10_10_26_488

Asda_2_0_Sustainability_Strategy_updated.pdf, Accessed: 20th May, 2012]

8. Asda Store Waste (2012) ' Cutting waste from our stores, depots and offices' Available at: http://your.asda.com/sustainability-store-waste, Accessed: 20th May, 2012]

9. Asda Sustainability Report (2007)

10. Asda Sustainability (2012) 'Fairtrade and Organic' : We care about Fairtrade and organic because you do' [Available at: http://your.asda.com/sustainability-fairtrade-and-organic/we-care-about-fairtrade-and-organic-because-you-do, Accessed: 13th August, 2012]

11. Asthma UK (2012) 'Shop at Waitrose and support Asthma UK'. [Available at: http://www.asthma.org.uk/news-centre/latest-news/2012/06/shop-at-waitrose-and-support-asthma-uk/, Accessed: 13th June, 2012]

12. Alzheimer's Society (2012) 'Alzheimer's Society chosen as one of Waitrose's national causes', [Available:http://www.alzheimers.org.uk/site/scripts/news_article.php?newsID=1233, Accessed: 13th June, 2012]

13. Bike Club (2012) 'Halfords Tour Series in Kirkcaldy' [A vailable at: http://bikeclub.org.uk/?s=asda&searchbutton=go%21, Accessed: 8th June, 2012]

14. Blowfield, M. and Murray, A. (2008) *Corporate Responsibility: a critical introduction*, Ist edn. Italy: Oxford University Press.

15. British Cancer Campaign (2012) 'Asda's Tickled Pink Campaign' [Available at: http://www.breastcancercampaign.org/page.aspx?pid=443, Accessed: 7th June, 2012]

16. BBC (2006) 'Supermarkets in Competition Probe'. [Available at: http://news.bbc.co.uk/1/hi/business/4753707.stm, Accessed: 12th June, 2012]

17. Carroll, A. B. (1991). The pyramid of corporate social responsibility: toward the moral management of organizational stakeholders. *Business Horizons, 34*(4): 39–48.

18. Cancer Research UK (2012a) ' Tesco Charity of the Year Internship' [Available at http://supportus.cancerresearchuk.org/volunteer/Internship-roles/Tesco-Charity-of-the-Year-Project-Internship-Volunteer-Fundraising/, Accessed: 10th June]

19. Cancer Research UK (2012b) 'Tesco collects used electric goods to benefit Cancer Research UK' [Available at: http://www.fundraising.co.uk/news/2012/06/21/tesco-collects-used-electrical-goods-benefit-cancer-research-uk, Accessed: 11th June]

20. Civil Society Fundraising (2011) 'Tesco supports women's health through feminine care products' [Available at: http://www.civilsociety.co.uk/fundraising/news/content/11590/tesco_launches_womens_health_charity_range_feminine_care, Accessed: 11th June]

21. Clean Air Power (2012) 'Duel-Fuel combustion technology enables Sainbury's delivery to 'Run on Rubbish' [Available at: http://www.cleanairpower.com/CAP_Sainsburys_dual-fuel_initiative.php, Accessed: 10th June, 2012]

22. Cooper, S. (2004) Corporate Social Performance: A Stakeholder Approach. Wiltshire: Ashgate.

23. Corporate Watch (2012) 'The argument against CSR' [Available at: http://www.corporatewatch.org/?lid=2688, Accessed: 13 August, 2012]

24. Crane, A., Matten, D. and Spence, L.J. (2008) Corporate Social Responsbility: Reaings and Cases in a global context. Oxon: Routledge.

25. Customer Insight (2011) 'Innovative Refrigerant Reduces Emissions, Enhances Energy Efficiency and Supports Sustainability.' [Available at: http://www51.honeywell.com/sm/chemicals/refrigerants/eu/en/common/documents/Performax_ASDA_CaseStudy_E_110630_final.pdf, Accessed: 20th May, 2012]

26. CTS Retail (2012) 'Waitrose to donate surplus food to charity' [Available at: http://www.cts-retail.com/waitrose-to-donate-surplus-food-to-charity/, Accessed: 12th June, 2012]

27. CSR Social Responsibility Report (2004) 'Waitrose'

28. Donaldson & Dunfee (1994) Towards a unified conception of business ethics: integrative social contracts theory. *Academy of Management Review*.vol:19, no:2

29. Davis, K (1960) 'Can Business affords to ignore Corporate Social Responsibilities'. *California Management Review*.vol:2

30. Edie Energy (2012) 'Waitrose advances towards off-grid with flagship energy centre'. Available at: http://www.edie.net/news/news_story.asp?id

=22190&title=Waitrose+advances+towards+off-grid+with+flagship+energy+centre, Accessed: 8th June, 2012]

31. Everyman (2012) 'Corporate Partnerships: Asda' Available: http://everyman-campaign.org/Get_Involved/Corporate_partnerships/corporate_partners/Adsa.shtml, Accessed: 8th June, 2012]

32. Ethical & Green (2012) 'Sainsbury's [Available at: http://ethicalandgreen.com/2007/10/17/sainsburys/, Accessed: 26th August, 2012]

33. Freight Transport Association (2011)
34. ASDA signs up to Logistics Carbon Reduction Scheme' [Available at: http://www.fta.co.uk/media_and_campaigns/press_releases/2011/20111010_asda_signs_up_to_logistics_carbon_reduction_scheme.html, Accessed: 20th May, 2012]

35. Food and Grocery Experts (2009) 'Waitrose –Reducing Waste' [Available at: http://www.igd.com/index.asp?id=1&fid=1&sid=5&tid=49&folid=0&cid=898, Accessed:9th June, 2012]

36. Farming UK (2007) 'ASDA ethical sourcing Head to address Anglesey farmers' [Available at: https://www.farminguk.com/news/ASDA-ethical-sourcing-Head-to-address-Anglesey-farmers_3404.html, Accessed: 13th May, 2012]

37. Fish Site (2009) 'Delivering Responsibly Sourced Lemon Sole to Asda' [Available at: http://www.thefishsite.com/fishnews/10353/delivering-responsibly-sourced-lemon-sole-to-asda, Accessed: 13th August,

2012]

38. First Milk (2012) 'Asda backs first milk to deliver regional cheese' [Available at: http://www.firstmilk.co.uk/media-centre/news/asda-backs-first-milk-to-deliver-regional-cheeses.html, Accessed: 13th August, 2012]

39. Galbreath, J (2009) 'Building Corporate Social Responsibility into

40. Strategy'.*European Business Review*.Vol : 21. Issue: 2. pp: 109-127

41. Garriga, Elisabet & Melé, Domènec (2004). Corporate social responsibility theories: Mapping the territory. *Journal of Business Ethics.* 53 (1)(2): 51-71. 1.

42. Graigner, J. S (2011) 'Ethical Labels Explained'. Verve Magazine. [Available at: http://stgr.net/196_Ethical_labels_explained.html Accessed: 18th May, 2012]

43. Gray, R., Bebbington, J. and Walters, D. (1993) *Accounting for the Environment*, Ist edn. London: Paul Chapman Publishing.

44. Greener Tesco (2012) 'Tesco automated recycling centres' [Available at: http://www.tesco.com/greenerliving/greener_tesco/what_tesco_is_doing/tesco_automated_recycling_centres.page, Accessed: 20th May, 2012]

45. Griseri, P & Seppala, N (2010) *'Business Ethics and Corporate Social Responsibility'*.Ist edn. Singapore: Cengage Learning

46. Grocer (2012) 'Sainsbury's donations total 100m for Active Kids'[Available at: http://www.thegrocer.co.uk/companies/sainsburys-donations-total-100m-for-active-kids/213035.article, Accessed: 19th May, 2012]

47. HU 17, (2012) 'Sainsbury's Make Donation to Beverly Primary School' [Available at: http://www.hu17.net/siansburys-make-donation-to-beverley-primary-school/, Accessed: 18th June, 2012]

48. Inside Games (2012) 'Record 100m Sainsbury's donation creating healthy, active kids' [Available at: http://www.insidethegames.biz/olympics/summer-olympics/2012/10751-record-p100m-sainsburys-donation-creating-healthy-active-kids, Accessed: 18th June, 2012]

49. Iles, A (2005) 'Seeing Sustainability in Business Operations: US and British Food Retailer Experiments with Accountability'. *Business Strategy & Environment.* Vol.16. 290-301.

50. John Lewis (2012a) 'Energy and Refrigeration' [Available at: http://www.johnlewispartnership.co.uk/csr/our-environment/energy.html, Accessed: 10th June, 2012]

51. John Lewis (2012b) 'Waste and Recycling' [Available at: http://www.johnlewispartnership.co.uk/csr/our-environment/waste-and-recycling.html, Accessed: 10th June, 2012]

52. Jones, P, C, Daphne, Hillier, D, Eastwood, I (2005) 'Retailers and Sustainable Development in the UK'. *International Journal of Retail & Distribution Management.* Vol.33. No:3

53. J Sainsbury PLC (2012a) 'Sainsbury's 20 by 20 Sustainability Plan' [Available at: http://www.j-sainsbury.co.uk/responsibility/20-by-20-commitments/#operational carbon, Accessed: 11th June, 2012]

54. J Sainsbury PLC (2012b) '1.2 Million meals donated to Fare Share' [Available at: http://j-sainsbury.co.uk/sainsburys-views/all-our-experts/andy-white/12-million-meals-donated-to-fareshare/, Accessed: 18th June, 2012]

55. J Sainsbury PLC (2012c) 'Sainsbury's outlines commitment to British Farming at Oxford Farming Conference' [Available at: http://www.j-sainsbury.co.uk/media/latest-stories/2012/20120103-sainsburys-outlines-commitment-to-british-farming-at-oxford-farming-conference/, Accessed: 28th August, 2012]

56. J Sainsbury PLC (2012d) 'Sainsbury's wins Good Farm Welfare accolades from Compassion in World Farming' [Available at: http://www.j-sainsbury.co.uk/extras/awards/2011/sainsburys-wins-good-farm-welfare-accolades-from-compassion-in-world-farming/, Accessed: 28th August, 2012]

57. J Sainsbury PLC (2012e) 'Responsibly Sourced Salmon' [Available at: http://www.j-sainsbury.co.uk/responsibility/case-studies/2011/responsibly-sourced-salmon/, Accessed: 28th August, 2012]

58. J Sainsbury PLC (2012f) 'Sainsbury's 20 by 20 Sustainability Plan' [Available at: http://www.j-sainsbury.co.uk/responsibility/20-by-20-commitments/, Accessed: 28th August, 2012]

59. Jobs Asda (2012) 'Community Projects' Available at:

http://www.asda.jobs/experienceAsda, Accessed: 8th[h] July, 2012]

60. Jones, P, Comfort,D, Hillier,D (2006) 'What's in store? Retail marketing and corporate social responsibility. *Market Intelligence and Planning*. vol.25. no.1

61. Keinert, C. (2008) Corporate Social Responsibility as an International Strategy. Heidelberg: Springer.

62. Louche, C., Idowu, S.O. and Filho, W.L. (2010) *Innovative CSR: From Risk management to Value Creation*. Sheffield: Greenleaf.

63. Luetchford, P. (2008) *Hidden Hands in the market*, Ist Edn. Bingley: Emerald.

64. Li, E (2008) 'Supermarket Chains and Grocery Market in UK'. *China Europe International Business School*

65. Mcintosh, M., Leipziger, D., Jones, K. and Coleman, G. (1998) *Corporate Citizenship: Successful Strategies for responsible companies*. Financial Times.

66. Muscliff Primary School (2012) 'Sainsbury's Castlepoint Charity Donation' [Available at:http://www.muscliffprimary.co.uk/index.php?option=com_content&view=article&id=132:sainsburys-castlepoint-charity-donation&catid=60:muscliff-parents-association&Itemid=81, Accessed: 18th June, 2012]

67. Mintel (2011) 'Food Retailing UK': Report Michaels, L (2004) 'What's Wrong With Supermarkets? Corporate Watch

68. Morgan, K & Morley, A (2002) 'Relocating the Food Chain: the Role of Creative Public Procurement. *The Regeneration Institute*, Cardiff University

69. Newton, L.H. (2005) Business Ethics & Natural Environment. Oxford.

70. Nidderdale Team (2012) 'Nidderdale AONB nominated as Waitrose Charity for September' [Available at: http://www.nidderdaleaonb.org.uk/nidderdale-468, Accessed: 15th June, 2012]

71. Ocado (2012) 'The Ocado Way' [Available at: http://www.ocado.com/theocadoway/being%20green/a-joint-effort.html, Accessed: 25th August, 2012]

72. Parliament UK (2012) 'Environmental Audit Committee: Written Evidence by Asda' [Available at:http://www.publications.parliament.uk/pa/cm201012/cmselect/cmenvaud/879/879vw21.htm, Accessed:13th August, 2012]

73. Procurement Leaders (2012) 'Asda creates ethical sourcing role' [Available at: http://www.procurementleaders.com/news-archive/news-archive/asda-creates-ethical-sourcing-role, Accessed: 13th August, 2012]

74. Rutland & Stamford Mercury (2012) 'Community Orchard Boosted by 200 donation from Sainsbury' [Available at: http://www.stamfordmercury.co.uk/news/local/community-orchard-boosted-by-200-donation-from-sainsbury-s-1-3823932, Accessed: 15th June, 2012]

75. RNIB (2002) 'RNIB sunshine House School unveiled as Sainsbury's South Ruslip New Local Charity

Partner' [Available at:http://www.rnib.org.uk/aboutus/mediacentre/mediareleases/mediareleases2012/Pages/pressrelease28june2012b.aspx, Accessed: 17th June, 2012]

76. Retail Week (2007) 'Asda to source an extra 270m of British food by 2013' [Available at: http://www.retail-week.com/in-business/responsible-retail/asda-to-source-an-extra-270m-of-british-food-by-2013/5018327.article, Accessed: 13th August, 2012]

77. Sainsbury's CSR Report (2011) 'Our values make us different'

78. Staib, R. (2005). *Environmental Management and Decision Making for Business.* Ist edn. Hampshire: Palgrave.

79. Tesco Magazine (2012) 'The Nature Choice' [Available at: https://secure.tesco.com/todayattesco/green/archive/0607_03_034_ggn_04.shtml, Accessed: 17th August, 2012]

80. Tesco CSR Report (2011) 'Achievements and Challenges'

81. Tesco Greener Living (2012) 'Using Greener Transportation' [Available at: http://www.tesco.com/greenerliving/greener_tesco/what_tesco_is_doing/greener_transportation.page, Accessed: 20th May, 2012]

82. Tesco Real Food (2012a) 'Tesco Farming' [Available at: http://realfood.tesco.com/our-food/tesco-farming.html, Accessed: 23th August, 2012]

83. Tesco Real Food (2012b) 'Tesco Beef Standards' [Available at: http://realfood.tesco.com/Our-Food/Tesco-Beef-Standards-.html, Accessed: 23th August,

2012]

84. Tesco Real Food (2012c) 'Tesco Egg Range' [Available at: http://realfood.tesco.com/Our-Food/The-Tesco-Egg-Range-.html, Accessed: 23th August, 2012]

85. Tesco Real Food (2012d) 'Tesco Chicken Range' [Available at: http://realfood.tesco.com/Our-Food/The-Tesco-Chicken-Range.html, Accessed: 23th August, 2012]

86. UK Fundraising (2012a) 'Tesco raises £7.5m for Alzheimer's Society and Alzheimer Scotland' [Available at: http://www.fundraising.co.uk/news/2012/04/26/tesco-raises-%C2%A375m-alzheimer039s-society-and-alzheimer-scotland, Accessed: 10 June, 2012]

87. Waitrose CSR Report (2011) 'A Clear View' – John Lewis Partnership

88. Waitrose Media Centre (2012a) 'World's First – Waitrose achieves highest ever BREEAM rating for a retail building'.[Available at: http://www.waitrose.presscentre.com/Press-Releases/World-first-Waitrose-achieves-highest-ever-BREEAM-rating-for-a-retail-building-8b8.aspx, Accessed: 9th June, 2012]

89. Waitrose Media Centre (2012b) 'Waitrose opens its lowest carbon store'. [Available at: http://www.waitrose.presscentre.com/Press-Releases/Waitrose-opens-its-lowest-carbon-store-yet-819.aspx, Accessed: 10th June, 2012]

90. Waitrose Media Centre (2012c) 'Waitrose launches Partner volunteering Scheme to donate 75,000 hours of time to good causes', Accessed: 13th June, 2012]

91. Waitrose Media Centre (2012d) 'Leckforth Produce' [Available at: http://www.waitrose.com/home/about_waitrose/our_company/leckford_estate/leckford_farm/leckford_produce.html, Accessed: 24th June, 2012]

92. Waitrose Inspiration (2012) 'LEAF' [Available at: http://www.waitrose.com/home/inspiration/food_issues_and_policies/farming/leaf.html, Accessed: 25th September, 2012]

93. Variety News (2012) 'Bring Some sunshine into the lives of Children this Summer' [Available at: http://variety.org.uk/section.php?id=18&article=107, Accessed: 13th June, 2012]

ABOUT THE AUTHOR

Naveed Qazi was born and brought up, in the Baghe Mehtab suburb, in Srinagar, Kashmir. He did his schooling, from Burn Hall School, and Tyndale Biscoe School.

After schooling, he pursued a Commerce degree, from Islamia College of Science & Commerce, Srinagar, affiliated to University of Kashmir. After that, he went on to pursue his master's degree in international business, from the University of Hertfordshire, in United Kingdom.

www.ingramcontent.com/pod-product-compliance
Lightning Source LLC
Chambersburg PA
CBHW070201230526
45471CB00002B/769